The Ocean of Love

At Sea – Dec: 11 —

My darling Leyla —

~~For you~~ – My ever faithful

Leyla — I have Nothing but

All My love

M° Grow

The *Ocean of Love*

My Life with Meher Baba

by Delia DeLeon

1991
SHERIAR PRESS

M.S. "MAJESTIC",

Published in the United States in 1991 by Sheriar Press, 3005 Highway 17 N. Bypass, Myrtle Beach, South Carolina 29577

Published in the United Kingdom in 1991 by Meher Baba Books, Old Rectory House, Marston Magna, Yeovil, Somerset BA22 8DT

DEDICATION

Baba is like the sun . . . anyone whose heart is pure can receive the rays. Make the heart pure by thinking of the Master, and then loving Him.

Baba is like the sea, which receives weak or strong, diseased or healthy, dotard, sinner or saint.

Baba is like an Infinite Ocean, and in order to realize Him the ego must be annihilated altogether.

MEHER BABA

These words, given by Meher Baba on the seashore at Combe Martin, Devon, on April 22, 1932, have inspired me to call my little tribute *The Ocean Of Love* dedicated to Beloved Meher Baba.

TABLE OF

CONTENTS

LIST OF
ILLUSTRATIONS

TREASURY OF CORRESPONDENCE

PROLOGUE

I have often marveled at the destiny which brought me to live in England, for I was born February 10, 1901 in Colon, on the Atlantic coast of the Isthmus of Panama. However, my cousins and I had an English governess and later several of us were sent to a boarding school in Jamaica run by three English ladies. My father had strong American links: his mother and sister lived in Cincinnati and he was in partnership with an American in an import-export business based in New York. It was therefore a surprising decision when in 1911 my parents brought us all to live and be educated in England as the more obvious choice would have been America. My father was to return to America only once after this in order to sell his business and sadly he died in 1914, leaving my mother a widow at thirty-six.

All my life I had had two intense desires—the first came to me when I was a child of about nine. Maybe it was the beauty of the warm tropical star-spangled nights in the West Indies that stirred my imagination to wonder what was beyond. My childish fancy came to picture God sitting on a throne just behind the stars. This started a train of thought in me that, though often dimmed, persisted. It gathered force and intensity as I grew older, leading to a deep desire to know and understand about God.

My second desire came later. I wanted to act—to be a great actress. Both desires ran parallel and were the pivot of my life. But the first one haunted me—I could not escape it.

I had the chance to travel a great deal, visiting Japan, Canada, USA, Honolulu, and many European countries and came to the conclusion, on seeing how akin human beings were the world over, that the mainly superficial differences between them could be easily overcome by good will and common sense. I mostly did as I liked, for I was spoiled and willful but, although I enjoyed life with its many experiences, deep down I was restless and dissatisfied and there still remained that deep thirst to know and understand about God.

Not being attracted to conventional forms of religion, I investigated "isms" and strange cults. I avidly read books and poems that told of mystical and spiritual experiences. I always remembered the stories heard in my childhood of Jesus and the holy women and Jesus especially attracted me—quite outside the church and religion with its rites and ceremonies.

It was not until 1931 that I was able to see where my life and my searching had been leading—to a particular moment in time when I was brought face to face with the one who was to become my Beloved Master. Indeed, on reflection, it was not strange when Meher Baba spelled out on the alphabet board, "It is not chance that brings you here!" This is how that meeting came about.

ACKNOWLEDGEMENTS

I have based these memoirs on those first published in THE GLOW in February 1974 for which many thanks to Naosherwan Anzar. I would like here to quote part of his introduction to that issue, as it may help those readers unfamiliar with Meher Baba to understand His methods.

> To the lay reader the account may give the impression that Baba spent a great deal of the time in England, Europe, and America, as the cynic would comment, in "frivolous activity". Such an impression would be grossly underrated, and in my view totally false. Meher Baba's unconventional working methods sprang precisely from the fact that He was able, with His divine knowledge, to capture latent states of mind and channel them to the benefits of the historical moment.

To these original memoirs I have added many of my articles

first published in *The Awakener* and the *Meher Baba Journal*, which I have expanded and augmented to bring up to date, as well as some entirely new material. I have included many of the letters sent to me by Meher Baba and it has been pointed out that those signed by Baba as "M.S. Irani", may be misinterpreted as they tend to be of a very personal nature. On the other hand many people have told me how valuable they found it reading them and so I have decided to leave in as many as I thought should be and, although I have edited some, I have been careful not to alter any of Baba's actual words.

However, I think a few words of explanation of how Baba worked with the first Western Disciples might help these letters be better understood in the spirit they were written, and I find I cannot improve on the explanation given by Manija S. Irani, Baba's sister, in a recent letter to me on the subject:

> Having sown the seed of His love in the hearts chosen for His spiritual universal work, He took such pains to nurture and strengthen the delicate plants in the early stages; He bestowed personal attention on each one according to individual needs until, as happened later on, the plants were strong enough to stand on their own and withstand the spiritual buffets that served to help in their tremendous growth and service to Him.

Lastly, as I did not feel at this stage in my life able to tackle the task of writing this on my own, I wish to express deep gratitude to Shireen Bonner who agreed, most lovingly, to help. Egged on by Kitty Davy, I suddenly felt the deep intuition to start and to enlist Shireen's help.

Special thanks also to Hilary Stabler for undertaking the arduous task of typing, revising, and amplifying the original text and to Mathew Price and Pete Townshend for all their advice and help.

Delia DeLeon

INTRODUCTION

Meher Baba influenced the spiritual lives of many thousands of people. He achieved this in various ways, but as far as I can tell He worked most powerfully—and poignantly—through the quietly demonstrative love of His followers.

Delia DeLeon was a follower of long standing when she influenced me and others who looked for spiritual truth during the '60s. It appeared that apart from her love for Him, her spiritual Master, she possessed and wanted nothing. He was her obsession. He was her absolute and singular focus. As I enjoyed a wonderful family and successful career when I first heard about Meher Baba such total devotion was impossible for me, but Delia DeLeon became an example and inspiration to me.

At times she seemed almost selfish in her driving commitment. As a composer I tried in vain to echo the endless love song that was her life, and felt embarrassed whenever she became impatient with me. It seems that it was Delia who Meher Baba chided with "Don't worry, be happy." Perhaps there are others who worry as much as she, but I doubt it. Her passion, constancy, meticulousness, and enormous anxiety have all blended to produce an endearing eccentricity that enriched my life. This has been possible because her tendency to worry—which she enjoys sharing with her helpers as much as possible—has always been tempered with the most extraordinary and mischievous sense of humor.

Through Delia I learned that Meher Baba calls first to the heart, then He tickles under the chin. It seemed this simple: let Delia do all the worrying! If I had looked more closely at the tribulations and exultations of Delia's life I would have been prepared for the deluge of joy and suffering that followed when later I properly opened my heart and made naive and impudent demands of Meher Baba as my own Master: the disciple does not choose but is chosen.

Meher Baba is the personification of pure love at a magnitude and power unimagined since the advent of Jesus. Reading Delia's story, so carefully told here, is like watching a tiny paper boat being swept away by the force of a massive hurricane.

Pete Townshend
Twickenham, England
January, 1990

ON THE THRESHOLD

After I left school I studied voice production and dramatic art, and even won the London Academy Gold Medal. Then along with my brother Jack, and his wife Beatrice, I started a school of acting. This did not last long and by 1931 we were in partnership again, managing and acting in a small experimental theater, sited at the foot of Kew Bridge in London, called the "Q" Theatre.

The "Q" Theatre was a pioneer of its type in England providing a place where little known dramatists and artists could perform. (Meher Baba was to visit there twice but sadly it has since been demolished.) This was part of a continuing connection I have had with Kew through the years: I went to boarding school there at Gloucester House and after the war moved back and have lived there now for the last forty years.

I was busy and happy at the theater. Acting under the stage name of Delia Delvina I took many parts—even going on tour for a short while. After many ups and downs, success did come to the "Q" Theatre, although it proved to be short lived.

At this time I used to buy a small weekly magazine called *The Everyman,* which was edited by Charles Purdom. In 1931, it carried a letter from Meredith Starr in reply to a letter in a previous issue that had bemoaned the fact that, despite the stress and upheaval of the modern world, so few people practiced meditation. Meredith described his recent stay with Meher Baba at Toka in India and also described a retreat he was running at East Challacombe.

I was intrigued by what Meredith had to say, cut the letter out and put it away.

Sadly by the summer of 1931, the "Q" Theatre had started to lose money. I had lost a lot of my own money and I had reached a point where I was at a very low ebb physically, mentally, and spiritually. It was at this psychological moment, having considered taking a trip abroad and deciding against it, that I opened a drawer and found Meredith's letter again. With a flash of intuition I knew that East Challacombe was where I should go. This feeling was so strong I knew nothing could prevent my going, and I immediately wrote to Meredith who arranged for me to visit the retreat.

East Challacombe was a converted 18th-century farmhouse outside the small village of Combe Martin, six miles from Ilfracombe, North Devon. There was no road leading to it, so having reached Combe Martin, I had to hire a boy to carry my luggage and show me the way. The farmhouse was set on the slope of a hill, and as I climbed I felt so exhilarated—was I not on the threshold of a strange and thrilling adventure?

The first person I met was Margaret Craske, out walking, having just finished a session of meditation. She took me by the hand and led me to the house where Meredith and his wife Margaret were waiting to welcome me.

Meredith, in his early forties, had a lively face and piercing eyes. He was an avid reader and the well-stocked library at the retreat was the pride of his heart. He had practiced meditation all his life and, although he was not destined to follow Baba for long, he was instrumental not only in telling the core of the early Western group about Baba, but also in bringing Meher Baba to Europe and America.

He had come to hear of Meher Baba in the following way. In 1927 he met Rustom Irani, a close disciple of Meher Baba, who had been sent to England to recruit boys for the Meherashram, a school Baba had opened a year earlier. In the school there were boys from mixed social and religious backgrounds and Baba wished the West to be represented there also, so he sent Rustom to see if any parents in England would be interested. Rustom placed the following advertisement in the English dailies:

A UNIQUE INSTITUTION

There is much talk about Brotherhood but not many attempts to make it practical have hitherto been made. A unique effort in this direction is now being made in India by Meher Baba, an Indian teacher whose reputation for wisdom and sanctity is well known throughout India. He has founded an institution known as Meherashram in Ahmednagar, not far from Poona. Admission to this institution is free to boys aged 10–16. Board, education, medical attention, and traveling expenses are all provided entirely free of charge for a period of two years. Boys of all races and creeds are welcome....

Yet Meherashram should not be considered a

charitable boarding school. It is open to rich and poor alike. Religious scruples are strictly respected. No attempt at conversion is made but the universal truths underlying all religion are taught, together with full secondary education....

> R. K. Sarosh Irani
> 36 Ashchurch Park Villas
> London W12

Not too surprisingly, Rustom failed to enroll any boys, but during his visit he did meet Meredith Starr. Meredith was very impressed by Rustom, saying that through him he felt the aura of his Master coming across the sea. On the strength of this feeling, he had the courage to ask if he could visit Baba in India. So, with Baba's approval, Meredith, his wife Margaret and sister Esther, went to visit the ashram in Toka for six months. After a happy stay, Baba sent them back to England, telling them to find somewhere where He could stay when He visited the West. He told Meredith He would guide him to the right property and at the right time He would come.

In July 1929, having acquired East Challacombe, Meredith wrote to Baba:

> I have tremendous faith in you and this faith increases daily—Please, dearest Baba, consider this house as your own. Come here whenever you like.

At the time of my visit to East Challacombe, the retreat had been in existence for two and a half years. It was run by Meredith and Margaret, helped by her brother Kenneth Ross, on simple, almost austere lines: four hours meditation a day; cold water to wash in; and vegetarian food. Visitors had to help out where needed, but there was still plenty of time for wonderful walks across the moors or in the beautiful countryside that surrounded it.

I took to this life like a duck to water. The farmhouse was very small and I remember that for the last week of my stay, Margaret and I had to sleep in the summerhouse in the garden. It did not matter. I felt so happy and carefree there and I must have gained immeasurably from my stay.

Margaret Craske and I got on from the first and have remained friends ever since. She was a ballet dancer, who had once worked with the Diaghilev Ballet, and was later appointed by Cecchetti as an exponent of his special technique of ballet training. When I first met her she was running a ballet school with her partner Mabel Ryan. I have always found in her great poise, serenity, and spiritual understanding.

Among the other people at the retreat while I was there was the scientist Thomas A. Watson, who had been a collaborator of Alexander Graham Bell. He was then seventy-eight years old and was there with his wife and a young protege, an American poet called Mylo Shattuck.

Kim Tolhurst (now Kim Grajera) and her husband came on a visit. Kim was a tall striking woman with auburn hair; half American on her father's side, she had two children. She wrote poetry and later developed a fine singing voice. We soon discovered that in fact we were neighbors, living on the same road in London, Compayne Gardens.

Also paying a visit was Charles Purdom, a man of many parts: accountant, author, critic, and at this time editor of *The Everyman* magazine through which I had come to hear about the East

Challacombe Retreat. He was there because he had started to correspond with Meredith over a series of articles he had been writing in *The Everyman* called A Plan for Life.

> My object in this series has been to give an outline of practical thoughts and action that would be of use to those who desire to get rid of the aimlessness of their lives. . . . When I started, I proposed to draw on my own experiences, using also the knowledge I had of what the philosophers have said and what religion has taught us. I had not, however, been in personal contact with a great Teacher, I did not know where such a Teacher was to be found. . . .

Being a practical mystic, Charles was a man of profound wisdom and I was to have a long association with him in organizing Baba activities in England.

During our stay Meredith lent us books from his library to read and he and his wife, both poets, would read their poems to us. Meredith had in fact had a book of poems published, *Arrows of Flame*, in which one of the poems was based on Baba's words, "You must become like dust at the feet of the Master."

SONG OF THE DUST
for SHRI SADGURU MEHER BABA

I am only the dust of his feet;
Let him tread me as much as he will.
Whatever they say, I repeat,
I am only the dust at his feet.
Dust has no will of its own,

Lies on the ground and is still,
Be the dust on the steps of a throne,
Or trodden by men in the street,
Or scattered by winds on the hill,
Dust is but dust, I repeat,
I am but the dust of his feet,
Slave of the slave of his will.

There is always some dust in the street
Where he walks to his work in the sun—
There is always some dust on the hill
Which he climbs when his labours are done.
I thrill to the kiss of his feet
As flowers thrill to the sun.

Trample me down as you will
I lie on the ground and am still,
I am but the dust of his feet,
Slave of the slave of his will.

Meredith also told his eager listeners stories of his stay in India and about the great Master. He said it was an experience he would not have missed for anything in the world—to quote his own words, "We only live to love and serve Him." His stories kindled in all of us a deep desire to meet Meher Baba. So it was a great thrill, while I was there on July 31, to hear of the arrival of the long-awaited cable from Baba announcing He was coming to the West. He had already delayed His visit, but now He was on His way and would be sailing on the Rajputana, which coincidentally was also carrying Mahatma Gandhi to a conference in London.

I had only planned a three-week stay at the retreat and so had to return to London, but as Meher Baba was going to be at East Challacombe for a year, I was going to arrange to return for a longer visit later in order to meet Him.

NOT BY CHANCE

When Meredith went to Marseilles to meet
Meher Baba he took with him a young man
called Herbert Davy. It was Herbert's older sister
Kitty who was to do stirring work for Baba in the
future, but at this time it was Herbert who was
the earnest seeker and who had told Kitty about
Meredith's retreat and taken her there in the spring of 1931.
When he met him, Meredith had been so impressed with Herbert
that he took him with him to welcome Baba off the boat. From
Marseilles the group traveled via Paris by train and boat to England. They stopped overnight at the house of Herbert's family at
32 Russell Road, Kensington, before traveling on to East Challacombe, stopping in Exeter for some time on the way.

As we were all to find out very soon, with Baba, plans were
always changing. Instead of staying at the retreat for a year, He
stayed just ten days before returning to London to stay once again
with the Davys at Russell Road.

After this sudden change of plans an appointment had been
made for me to meet Him at Russell Road the day after His return,
but the very evening they arrived, Margaret, who had been

at East Challacombe with Him, rang me up. Baba wanted to go to the theater and a box had been booked at the Coliseum for a musical comedy called "The White Horse Inn." Margaret wanted me to come to the theater as they had promised Baba a surprise, and I was to be that surprise.

I had imagined what the scene would be like when I first met Baba—a solemn atmosphere with me falling, weeping at the feet of the Christ. But Baba was teaching me the first of many, many lessons before I even met Him. With His humanness and His humor, He was showing me how false an idea of true spirituality this was.

I had been instructed that when I saw Baba arrive at the theater I was to wait at the box office and not to go up and talk with the group. So I stood while they passed—Baba wearing a long English coat and a hat down to His nose—and disappeared into the box. Soon afterward Meredith arrived and it was he who showed me into Baba's presence. By this time Baba had taken off His coat and hat, allowing His hair to fall to His shoulders. Someone said, "This is your surprise, Baba!" He looked at me kindly, made me sit next to Him, and patted my hand. From that moment I intuitively recognized Him as my Master and I suddenly wanted to cry.

I was stunned. I had seen His face before in my dreams: the eyes were startling in their beauty; the face seemed luminous, honey-colored, framed by a halo of long, dark hair. He seemed to be enjoying the play; there was a funny man in it and I heard Baba chuckling. Other than that I hardly heard or saw anything because I was only conscious of Baba sitting there. At the end I could only look at Him and say, "Baba, I must see You again," and He nodded.

It was only many years later, I came to realize the full signifi-

cance of the play, "The White Horse Inn," for Baba is known as
the "White Horse" or "Kali" Avatar by His Hindu followers. Even
the plot of the play had significance which I did not fully appreciate until 1980, when I went on my own to see a revival at the
Richmond Theatre. The first time I had been too absorbed in Baba
to pay it any attention. Set in an inn in Austria where everybody
and everything is at sixes-and-sevens, it tells how the Emperor pays
a visit, sorts everything out, and settles all quarrels.

I went home after this first meeting with Baba in a dream.
That night I kept thinking of Him and I slept very little. The next
morning, still in a daze, and much to the astonishment of my
family, I rushed off with Kim at—what was for me—an incredibly
early hour to Russell Road for my first interview.

It was there that I met Kitty Davy for the first time. A piano
teacher, she had had many spiritual experiences and had already
given her life to Baba. From the start her chief concern was Baba's
comfort and pleasure and I have always been touched by the way
she mothered our little group in those early days, always bubbling
and rushing around looking after us. I've always admired too her
capacity for hard work and her willingness to take on new chal-
lenges if she thought they would help with Baba's work, such as
learning typing and languages.

In 1925 Meher Baba had started observing silence and was,
when I met Him, communicating by means of an alphabet board
which, as we found it difficult, was usually carried and read by His
secretary, F. H. Dadachanji, known as Chanji. But for my first
interview I was alone with Him. He embraced me and I sat next to
Him—again His love swamped me. I did not feel He was silent; He
was speaking to my soul. Then He spelled out on the board, "It is
not chance that brought you here."

Baba was in London for a week and I went with Kim every day to Russell Road to see Him. On this first visit, He had brought with Him three of His Indian disciples who were with Him constantly: Rustom, who had already been to England and who became great friends with Herbert; Chanji, who became a firm favorite with us all, because, although he was Eastern, he understood us and became like an uncle to us and through his tales we were able to glean a little of what life was like with Baba in India and how people behaved with him; and little Ali, a pupil at the Prem Ashram, a section of the Meherashram where the boys were given additional spiritual training. The stories of Ali's determination to stay with his Master at the school, in spite of his family's opposition, were heart-warming. He was a good-looking seventeen-year-old, full of humor. He took a special liking to Kim and separated her out and thus christened the English group by announcing on our arrivals, "Baba, Keem and Co. are here!" Baba was soon referring to us under the collective name of "Kimco."

Many others came to see Baba in that first week. I brought my mother, my brother, Jack, and my sister, Minta. In fact, all my family were to meet Baba. On the whole they were skeptical and did not understand about Baba and His silence but they were very patient and accepted my need to be with Him and obey His orders. Minta, however, did recognize Baba for what He was. When she first saw Him sitting cross-legged on a bed, it seemed to her as she approached that He was full of light and she fell weeping at His feet. She was to be close to Baba for the first few years and He took so much notice of her that I became quite jealous. This was one of Baba's little pricks to show me that I was capable of jealousy, for up to that time I had prided myself that I was never jealous.

At this time, Margaret brought her friend, Quentin Tod, to

see Baba. He had enormous charm; he loved Baba and above all he was able to keep Him amused. He and his brother, Kenneth, did music hall turns and he had worked for Andre Charlot as a producer so he had a host of theatrical and film contacts which were useful when he traveled to America with Baba. Quentin and Herbert Davy were complete opposites—one supplied what the other lacked—but they were both important elements in those early years in Europe. Sadly Quentin was to die soon after World War II.

Another early follower brought by Margaret was her partner Mabel Ryan, who had originally come all the way from South Africa to study with her and at this time they were running a dancing school together near Cambridge Circus in London. She was a lovable person, full of humor, always calling Baba "my boy."

Despite all this activity and visits, everything and everyone faded from my mind except Baba. He alone seemed real—the perfect human being. His love melted me and as I became gradually more and more aware of His sense of humor, His humor and charm attracted me. He was silent but it never seemed that He did not speak—His silence was more potent than words.

> I am never silent, I speak eternally. The voice that is heard deep within the Soul is My voice, the voice of inspiration, of intuition, of guidance.

When I looked at the people passing in the streets I thought, "Baba is in the world and they do not know it. How strange that this should be happening to me." As the poor barber said of his meeting with the Buddha:

The Blessed One passed by my house,
My house, the barber's.
I ran, and He turned and awaited me,
Me, the barber.
I said, "May I speak, O Lord, with thee?"
And He said, "Yes."
Yes, to **me**, the barber!
And I said, "Is the Peace for such as I?"
And He said, "Yes."
Even for **me**, the barber!
And I said, "May I follow after thee?"
And He said, "Yes."
Even **I**, the barber!
And I said, "May I stay, O Lord, near thee?"
And He said, "Thou mayest."
Even to **me**, the poor barber.

Of necessity the first meeting with one's master in the flesh is a cataclysmic experience. For it shakes us to our very foundations on all levels of our conscious and unconscious selves, and what the master sets in motion goes on bearing fruit even if not apparent to ourselves or to others. In this freeing process all our latent qualities, both good and bad, are brought to the surface and our whole being is quickened and geared up to a new level of consciousness in which the master becomes the focal point of lives.

Kim was interested in Buddhism, and had brought the president of the Buddhist Society, Judge Christmas Humphreys, to see Baba. Of this first meeting he commented:

For the first time in my life, and I have not met another

like Him, I found myself in the aura of a man who literally radiated love...He combined the profundity of mystical experience with the guileless candour of a child, and His smile was as infectious as the words He used were immaterial. And all the while He radiated such a pure affection that one wondered why, when all religions praise the value of pure love, it should be a memorable experience to meet one man who practiced it. If there were more Meher Babas in the world today war would end for want of causes. This man of love sets all men an example.

And Charles Purdom, writing in his magazine:

I have been brought by what seems chance, but no doubt deserves some other name, into a personal contact with a Perfect Master, from the East...His eyes are large and beaming, lighting up His face which irradiates happiness. He has a great sense of fun and is said to be a first rate cricketer. He combines the simplicity of a child with the wisdom of the ages...I have had several conversations with Him. But, as I have said, to talk with Him is not the important matter. It is sufficient to be in the same place...to know the truth. He does not need to speak: He has the power of truth in Him. The way to truth is simple but it is very hard, for the way to know God is to know oneself, to face oneself in one's own inner consciousness and then, renouncing everything, to let God flood the soul...Meher Baba is master of one knowledge which is God, but that knowledge includes everything else...He has no doctrine, He is the living truth.

For me it was a wonderful experience to be in Baba's radiant presence. When He enfolded me in His loving arms and His eyes gazed deeply into mine, I knew that my search was over. I loved Him and believed in Him and gave my life into His keeping. The week of His first stay in London went like a dream, and on the last night as we all sat round Him listening to records of Paul Robeson singing such Negro spirituals as "Steal Away To Jesus" and "Is There Anybody Here Like Weeping Mary," He looked so beautiful and so sorrowful. We all wept at the imminence of His departure but He promised to be with us again soon.

THE GENTLE BEGINNING

 In the early days we saw Baba every few months and in between there were cables and general and individual letters. These letters were full of love and thought for all of us: sometimes chiding, giving advice or orders; but always gentle and patient with us, His erring children. Most of them were written by Chanji along guidelines given by Baba but the first few letters I received were from Ali, the first from Istanbul.

> Hotel Continental
> 58 Bld des Petits-Champs
> Pera, Istanbul
> le 13 Octobre 1931

Dear Delia,

　　Just received your letter. I know how dearly you love Me and how you long to do My will.

　　I am ever present in your own self.

Goodbye till we meet again.

With love, yours,
BABA

Baba traveled from Istanbul through Milan to Genoa from where He sailed for New York:

Milan
24th October 1931

Dear Delia,

Your love for Baba will one day make you long to become merged in His Ocean of Divinity...We are leaving Italy October 27 for New York on S.S. ROMA.

From the first Baba emphasized that, although England had an important part to play in His work, America—the synthesis of so many races—would be the scene of the great spiritual revival and He said He would direct its enormous energy into the right channels. It is quite clear that all of us destined to belong to that early group in America and England were found and linked in an indissoluble bond.

The pioneering work in America was carried out with eager anticipation by Malcolm and Jean Schloss. They were running a book shop in New York and had come in contact with Meredith Starr through his book of poems, *Arrows of Flame*. Malcolm was also a poet and he and Meredith exchanged books by post. The Schloss' were planning to come over to East Challacombe to meet Baba but Meredith sent Milo Shattuck back to America to stop them and tell them to make preparations as Baba was coming to

America. They set about these arrangements enthusiastically, creating a center at Harmon-on-Hudson for Baba's visit.

During the month that Baba was away in America I continued working at the "Q" Theatre and I was often with Kim. We became great friends and started work on a spiritual anthology to be dedicated to Baba. We bought books and spent two or three days a week at the library doing research. Although it never came to anything (what there is of it, is at the Myrtle Beach Center), we did learn a great deal and it kept us busy and thinking about Baba in His absence.

All the time we were in touch with the rest of Kimco and with Baba in America through letters:

> Hotel Astor
> New York
> 28 November 1931

> We are leaving New York for Harmon tonight and we are sailing from New York for India on December 6th, S.S. Bremen. It is now a good chance for you— staying seven days Paris and seven days Egypt and sailing Port Said on December 30th, S.S. Rampura arriving Bombay 8/1/32.

> Our Beloved Baba sends His love to you dear. He is always with you, in you, and near you, and He says, "Be happy," and not to worry....

> *Ali*

How excited we were to get the call on December 11th to go to Paris for the meeting hinted at by Ali in this letter. As well as Baba,

Chanji, Ali, and the Starrs from America, there was Kitty, her niece Zilla, a little boy called John Cousins, Margaret, Kim, and myself.

After a while Baba told Meredith that, at his stage of development, the heavy occult atmosphere in Paris was not good for him and sent him and his wife, Margaret, home. When we heard, Kim and I took this very seriously and sat up all night quoting spiritual passages from the Bible and any other spiritual discourses we could think of. I can still see the look of utter disgust on Margaret's face when we told Baba, rather smugly the next morning, that we thought this would help Him clear the atmosphere. Baba, on the other hand, looked delighted and patted us on the back.

When the Starrs had left, Baba was in a lighter, holiday mood. We went sightseeing to Versailles and went to the cinema to see Charlie Chaplin and Laurel and Hardy. He also spent time playing games such as tiddlywinks and marbles with young John Cousins.

With all of us Baba was so sweet and patient, treating us like the children we were, while all the time doing His Universal Work. Although we did not know it, this was the gentle beginning of our training in discipleship. His Indian disciples must have been appalled at the way we treated Him. In our innocence we behaved with a spontaneity and a light-heartedness, treating Him as if He were one of us, which was the complete opposite of what they were used to. From my point of view I did not realize the implications of Baba's Universal Work and was unaware of any training. I loved Him and I wished only to be with Him and do whatever He wanted.

After a few days Kim and I returned to London with the promise that we would see Baba again soon. We were particularly sad at being sent home while Margaret was allowed to go to Marseilles to see Him off on the boat for India, but we were not to be sad for long because three months later, on April 9, 1932, Meher Baba arrived in England for the second time.

BEADS ON ONE STRING

 As Kitty's parents were away, Kimco invited Baba to stay once again at the Davy home in Russell Road. Kim, Margaret, and I stayed there with Him. It was on this occasion that He delivered the message to the West which was read by Charles Purdom from the alphabet board and filmed by Paramount News Reel in the back garden at Russell Road:

My coming to the West is not with the object of establishing new creeds of spiritual societies or organizations, but is intended to make people understand religion in its true sense. I intend to bring together all religions and cults like beads on one string and revitalize them for individual and collective needs.... The book which I shall make people read is the book of the heart, which holds the key to the mystery of life.

This was a most important event, as it was the first time the

Avatar had been filmed; people all over the world, then and in the future, would be able to see Him in action. In fact, Baba said that in times to come people would gain illumination by seeing Him on the screen.

The close disciples who lived with Baba in India were known as the *mandali*. This time Baba had brought seven of the *mandali* with Him, among them His brothers Adi, Behram, and Jal, as well as Adi Sr., Chanji, Kaka, and Dr. Ghani.

The days were full of interviews and there were excursions to see the sights: we visited the British Museum; I remember Baba riding up and down on the escalator at Piccadilly Circus; and there was also a lovely day spent in Kew Gardens where we had a picnic lunch. In the evenings there was entertainment. During the previous months we had rehearsed a sketch about a country Post Office, and while we were at the Davy house we performed it for Baba. He seemed amused which made us very happy; and we in our turn enjoyed Eastern music performed by the *mandali*.

Baba liked entertainment: He loved comedians and anything with vitality and verve, such as Spanish dancing, Charlie Chaplin, Laurel and Hardy, and Fatty Arbuckle films. I had had a few lessons on the ukulele and one night I performed "Santa Lucia" for Him, accompanied by Kim on guitar. He was a most appreciative audience and anyone who has performed for Him will know the feeling of exhilaration it gives. But as everything He did had meaning and purpose, it was obvious that on these occasions He must have been working on a deeper level of the consciousness of the individual.

Not being aware at that time of Baba's ways of working we were a little puzzled when, at the most awkward moments, He would ask us, "What are you thinking?" We tried to be truthful, and, of course, He already knew our innermost thoughts, but He used this method to release many hidden problems. It was one more way of making us conscious of our unacknowledged thoughts.

There was much press attention during this visit and as a result many new people came to see Him, among them two people who were destined to have a very special role in the British group, Will and Mary Backett—Baba soon came to call them by the collective name "Wilmar." They were both Sufis, Mary having studied under Inayat Khan himself. They made a sweet couple. Will's serious nature contrasted with Mary's great sense of fun. They both had an old world charm about them. Mary, in particular, wove and made her own clothes and looked as if she had stepped straight out of the Bible. She had only agreed to marry Will as long as their relationship remained platonic; and they lived a simple life in the country, creating in their home such a warm loving atmosphere that people would flock to be with them there and hear about Baba. Of their first meeting with Baba, Mary writes:

> He was seated in a small room at the top of the house surrounded by some close devotees. They did not hear me enter, but Baba sprang up with agility, power, and grace that characterized all His movements and came quickly forward. He then signed me to sit by Him and took my hand with the gentle touch we know so well.
>
> Immediately I felt a great upliftment of consciousness such as I had never experienced with anyone before...He gave me more, far more in the space of three minutes than I had gained in thirty years of

earnest seeking or through others because I experienced the tangible definite gift of grace and Divine
Love that He bestowed, whereas others only talk about
it. I know who Baba is.

And Will:

Many first impressions lose their keenness as time
passes, but this meeting with Baba stands out clearer in
my consciousness as my subsequent experiences enable
me to appreciate more completely the significance of
such a contact with Him. Looking back, I can see Baba
seated quietly on a settee, that it might appear to the
casual observer that He lacked energy, yet there was
something compelling in His posture, for the picture
stands out like a cameo in my mind, pure and untram-
meled by the world, completely poised like a bird
arrested momentarily in flight, in a world that reflects
not the like anywhere.

Before He left, Baba kept a promise to Kim and stayed for two
days at her home in Compayne Gardens. On one of the days we
took Him to see Charlie Chaplin in "Goldrush," which He loved. I
was sent back in advance to prepare a meal. I had never cooked rice
before and I got into a panic thinking I had not done enough and
kept adding more to the saucepan—I imagine half of it was
uncooked. Baba beamed when they arrived back and said He was
hungry. He was given a portion but what happened to it I don't
know, not a word was said to me. Such is Baba's kindness when you
try your best.

There were many other little personal things through which He brought us closer: I remember once watching Him dunking His bread in His tea. He mischievously looked up and asked, "Is it done?" I replied, "No, Baba, but I do it." And I admit I still do when no one is looking.

In the meantime a large crowd had gathered at East Challacombe waiting for Baba's second visit, among them Quentin Tod, Mabel Ryan, Minta and a friend, and Tom and Hugh Sharpley. Tom was very involved for a while. He was a very neurotic young man with his own complex problems—physical and mental—and a bizarre lifestyle, sleeping all day and staying awake all night. By the time Kitty, Margaret, Kim, and I had arrived with Baba and the *mandali* from London, it was so full that the men had to sleep in the stables.

The scene at that remote farmhouse, thronging with eager questing souls, was reminiscent of the New Testament. Watching Baba giving interviews and walking among His lovers showering His love on all was an incredible and illuminating experience.

Meredith had insisted on keeping to the usual daily practice of a meditation hour. Although Baba had said we need not meditate, He would come and sit with us during this time. One day He pulled a book from the bookshelf and showed us the title: *All Quiet on the Western Front.* Then, as we were about to giggle, with a twinkle in His eye He put His finger to His lips. One of the most endearing qualities about Baba was this sense of humor.

Later Baba was to tell us we were not to go back to East Challacombe because of Meredith's drive for power, and so this was the last time we were there. Although there have been two or three serious attempts made to buy it since and reestablish it as a retreat for Baba, these have not materialized.

A TRYING TIME

Baba had announced that He wanted a holiday before going to America again and Lugano in Switzerland was selected. Kim, Kitty, Minta, Margaret, and I were to go with Him and the *mandali* and rooms were booked at the Eden Hotel. I was sent back to London in advance of the main party to ask Kim's husband, Desmond, if she could come with us. Their marriage was going through some problems, and Desmond only agreed to Kim's coming with us after Baba sent him a cable promising that He would see that their relationship improved if he allowed her to come.

On the boat during the journey over to the Continent, we noticed Baba several times cover His face with a white cloth. He said He was holding a spiritual meeting. Because of the cloth, we could not see His face, but we sometimes saw His fingers moving as if He were signing something.

At the time, this Lugano period was a complete puzzle to me. I seemed to be groping in the dark, trying to understand what Baba was trying to do; why He stirred in us emotions that we hardly knew or would not admit we possessed, but which were obviously deeply rooted in our natures. Jealousy, greed, pride, and meanness were brought to the surface. As we spent more time with Baba through the years, we realized that this was one of His ways of working, by wearing down the ego. He was treating me with apparent indifference, seeming to use me as a buffer between Kim and Minta, who were both determined to be the first and foremost disciple. Just before He left, however, He did console me, telling me that I had been very patient and had helped Him with His work.

Margaret also had a bad time but she, as always, was a tower of strength in her understanding of Baba. She managed to keep her level-headedness and humor under the most trying circumstances; like the time, during one of the many excursions, when Baba called her to do a dance in a cafe on the top of a mountain.

At the most awkward times, He would demand radishes, cheese, or potato chips. Kitty was indefatigable, coming through these tests with flying colors. To our astonishment, she always seemed able to succeed; once she rushed into a house while the funicular railway was making a brief stop and demanded radishes; at another time she went into one of the best hotels in Lugano late at night to ask for potato chips! She subsequently capped this by cabling Quentin to send out several packets by air.

On one of the lake excursions a very interesting old man sat opposite Baba and kept tapping his stick on the deck of the boat. Afterward, Baba explained that this old man was an agent on the third plane and that during their meeting Baba had raised him to the fourth. He went on to tell us many things about His Circle and about the evolutionary plan for unconscious divinity to conscious divinity. Unfortunately, Minta seemed to think this very funny and burst out laughing, which spoiled Baba's mood, much to the *mandali's* disgust. Along with the rest of us they were already having a hard time; I think it was at this time Baba made them eat fish which, as they were vegetarians, was difficult for them.

And then Kim threw a tantrum and rushed off. We were all sent to look for her and found her in a church weeping at the foot of the altar. We did not know it then, but this was the last time she was to be with Baba, for the promise He had made to Desmond to help their marriage meant that after this she drifted away.

So we all had a trying time in various ways. Baba was working on us all and for us all, knowing just what each one needed for his or her development. We were all in a curiously exhausted state. It was as if one had lived through a lifetime in this short period. We soon learned that this is a usual experience among Baba's disciples, for it is in this emptied state that Baba can best work on the subconscious. Usually after this emptying process a renewed vitality is felt as if a purging and burning up of the dross has taken place. In psychological terms it is called catharsis, and often brings the patient back to health and normality. It is in this "let go" state that one is more receptive to the love and truth the master wishes to give.

Something of our state when we arrived back in London was sensed by Quentin who met us at Victoria Station and noted in his diary:

> Baba was met by Meredith and Margaret Starr, who by their attitude seemed determined to exercise what they thought was their proprietary right over Him. He left Victoria Station flanked by them both, like two policemen. The girls arrived back stunned and tired

which is usual after being with Baba. The visit seems to have been one of mixed pleasure....

The Starrs were making themselves increasingly unpopular, and soon after this they left Baba, eventually becoming disciples of Subud. Meredith died in 1970, but his courage, intuition, and tenacity of purpose which made him such a fitting vehicle for the Avatar to use as His first link with the West, should not be forgotten.

At the station on the way back from Lugano, Baba had said He would like a dog to take to America. While He stopped off in Paris, we decided to see about getting one for Him and arranged for several to be sent to the hotel when we returned to London. We were shocked, however, to find that the price of the one He liked was £100.

Chanji told Baba, who immediately told us we must send this one back and get a cheaper one. So Quentin went the next day and brought back an untrained mongrel which we called "Mikko" after our group "Kimco." Baba kept the dog for a night or so, then the day before He left for America, much to my horror, He told me He was leaving Mikko behind and that I was to take care of him.

At first, being untrained, Mikko was a great trial but soon the whole family grew fond of him. However, he caused me continual alarm as he was always developing some ailment that needed treatment. It was probably my complete inexperience with animals that made me worry so much, as we had never had any in our home—not even a kitten. And, thankfully, soon after Baba wrote, "Don't worry if anything happens to Mikko!"

MESSAGE TO BEVERLY HILLS

This time in America Baba referred to the breaking of His silence which He said He would definitely do by July 13, and He re-emphasized what He had said in England:

> I have not come to establish any cult, society, or organization, nor even to establish a new religion. The religion I shall give teaches the knowledge of the one behind the many—the book that I shall make people read is the book of the heart which holds the key to the mystery of life.

> New York, May 19, 1932

And again in New York:

> My work and aims are intensely practical. It is not practical to overemphasize the material at the cost of the spiritual. It is not practical to have spiritual ideals without putting them into practice. But to realize the

ideal in daily life, to give beautiful and adequate form to the living spirit, to make brotherhood a fact not merely a theory as at present, this is being practical in every sense of the word.

We were kept in touch with events in America through letters from Quentin. He had many theatrical contacts and was able to bring many film stars to meet Baba while they were in Hollywood. They visited several studios meeting producers and actors, among them Gary Cooper, Marlene Dietrich, Ernst Lubitsch. Talullah Bankhead was very drawn to Baba and came several times to see Him. Of all the stars, Baba said, Greta Garbo was the most spiritual and He expressed a wish to meet her; but although Talullah Bankhead tried several times to arrange a meeting, it did not come about.

A large reception was given for Baba at the Knickerbocker Hotel where a thousand people were present; one can only imagine what work He did on this crowd for the future development of the arts. At another reception given at Pickfair by Douglas Fairbanks and Mary Pickford, Baba gave His "message to Beverly Hills," stressing the responsibilities of those concerned with the theater in general and the film world in particular:

> I do not need to tell you, who are engaged in the production and distribution of moving pictures what a power you hold in your hands, nor do I doubt that you are fully alive to the responsibility which the wielding of that power involves. He who stimulates the imagination of the masses can move them in any direction he chooses and there is no more powerful instrument for

stimulating the imagination than the moving picture. People go to the theater to be entertained.... Plays which inspire those who see them to greater under-standing, truer feeling, better lives, need not necessarily have anything to do with religion.

Real spirituality is best portrayed in stories of pure lives, selfless service, of truth realized and applied to the most humble circumstances of our daily lives... This is the highest practicality. To portray such circumstances on the screen will make people realize that the spiritual life is something to be lived, not talked about and that it—and it alone—will produce the peace and love and harmony which we seek to establish as the constant rule of our lives.

This made it clear the part that Baba wished the film industry to play both then and in the future in helping awaken people to the true meaning and purpose of life.

Of course, as usual, there were changes of plans. We soon came to realize this was part of Baba's technique to test the loyalty and staying power of His followers. At this time it certainly put a great strain on His American followers. He said that before He broke His silence in Hollywood it was necessary for Him to visit China and He therefore left California for Honolulu on June 4. All general letters addressed to Kimco at this time were sent to Kitty but there were still individual ones, and I received one from the Moana Hotel, in which coincidentally I had stayed in 1919. As usual it was written by Chanji on guidelines given by Baba.

Moana Hotel
Honolulu
June 10th, 1932

Dear Delia,

Baba received your letters. There is no need to explain to you how pleased He was to read those lines—rather through the lines—as He feels and knows how you love, long, and feel for Him. Expression and demonstration of these feelings and love are not necessary for Him who knows all. You suffered silently even when He was there physically with and among you all, and how intensely you will be suffering the painful separation; He knows, and loves you all the more for that. For this intense longing and pangs of separation you get nearer and dearer to Him every moment, and you always remain in His thoughts as He remains in yours. And nothing is more desirable. You have really deserved every thought that He has been giving you, and He is so pleased with you for that.

And now He instructs me to write to you to say that *He wants to see you all* in August, and keep you with Him thereafter. But meanwhile you are to act as He wishes and as explained in the last general letter to Kimco, read that letter and act accordingly. Most of all He wishes you *not at all to worry* for any abrupt change in His plans or program of His working.

And now a few more words from Baba: that He always marked His dear sweet Delia keeping herself away or aloof to give a chance to others to go near Him, though wishing in her heart of hearts to be always in

His fond, warm embrace; and suffering silently as self-less love alone could enable one to suffer, ever ready to pick up His word and work for Him. When He remembers all this, tears appear in His eyes and the expression on His face would show how deeply He thinks of someone who loves Him with all her heart; and it is such a satisfaction, such a delight, for us to see and know how richly you deserve every thought of His heart, every drop of His eyes.

With more and more of His love.

With loving regards,
Yours, *Chanji*

Please deliver the enclosed letter to <u>Minta</u> personally.

The news that we might be with Baba indefinitely delighted me as I wanted to be with Baba always, not realizing that this was an escape mechanism on my part to get away from being in the world and living in an integrated manner.

Herbert was already in China. He had been offered a position there and, with Baba's approval, had taken it; so he was in Shanghai to receive Baba and the group when they arrived on June 22.

Shanghai
June 27, 1932

My darling Delia,
You must have read the diary of events written by Chanji for Kimco.
We arrived Shanghai on the 22nd and were received on the boat by Kitty's brother, Herbert. After a day and

a half in Shanghai, we went to Nanking and stayed at Herbert's for a few days. We stayed in all about a week in China, and all these seven days Herbert was constantly with us.

I am sending Herbert to London via Liberia. He will reach England on 24th July. I am coming via Marseilles to Genoa where I will arrive on 29th July. You, Herbert, and Kimco (except Kim) will come to meet Me in Genoa on the 29th.

I know you remember and think of Me continually and are counting the days when you will meet Me again. And you have a permanent place in My heart. We'll have a personal heart-to-heart talk when we meet in Genoa. Till then try to have patience.

> With My greatest love,
> BABA

N.B. Give the enclosed to Kim and Minta.

(Writer's note: As Chanji has gone out with Herbert on Baba's errands, I am writing this letter at Baba's order.)

> *Little Adi*

"Little" Adi was Baba's youngest brother. Needless to say we were delighted at the prospect of staying with Baba in Europe again.

ITALIAN HOLIDAY

 I think that it would be unanimous that this Italian holiday with Baba gave us some of our loveliest moments with Him because it was the most carefree and happy time I had with Baba; He was in holiday mood, it was summer, and the surroundings were delightful.

Apart from Baba, Chanji, and Kaka, there were Quentin, Herbert, Mabel, Margaret, Kitty, Minta, and Audrey Ince, who was a young and beautiful student of Margaret's. Baba had met her when He visited Margaret's studio in London and said she had to make contact with India and we were to bring her with us when we came.

We stayed at the Villa Fiorenza, a small pension between Santa Margherita and Portofino, which we had to ourselves—apart from one English couple who were in the annex—and where we ate our meals on a picturesque veranda facing the sea. Every morning Baba came round our rooms to see that we were up and teased and embraced us. Then most mornings, followed by Kaka with a large umbrella, Baba came down to the beach and sat on the rocks while some of the group went swimming. He told us that for spiritual reasons He would not go in the water Himself.

While we sat on the beach, many Italians attracted by this strange group would come and sit near us. We must have presented a queer picture, an Indian with long hair and flowing white robes followed by a group of men and Western women in colorful attire; but the Italians are a marvelous people, they never stared but took it as a most natural sight.

In the evenings, we listened to Hawaiian, Spanish, or Paul Robeson records; or we were called upon to give impromptu concerts or tell funny stories; but among my most precious recollections was when we just sat in silence with Baba on the terrace—no one saying a word—the silence broken only by the lapping waves. One evening in particular, I remember following Him onto the terrace. The moon was shining straight onto His face and, as we sat around Him in silence, we could feel Him drawing us closer in love. Chanji told us that few in India had been permitted this degree of intimacy, and Baba Himself told us, "Make the most of this—it won't come again—one day you won't get near me for the crowds!"

One evening, for the first time, He told us of the Eastern women *mandali* and of His love for Mehera and of her great beauty. Some say that Mehera represents *Mâyâ* to Baba, and others that she represents His feminine aspect and spiritually He works on all femininity through her. Certainly He has always said that, while others are very near and dear to Him in varying degrees, she is "the Chosen One." In Portofino, He said that we loved Him the same way and that we would always have a special place in His heart. He said He was training us for the work we had to do in the future and that everything that He said would come to pass.

Once we were discussing books and Baba said, "Learn to read me then you will understand everything." And on another occasion He described the Circle of the Avatar and gave us Persian names to please us: Delia – Leyla; Minta – Shalimar; Kitty – Saroja; Margaret – Zuleka; Audrey – Shirin; Kim – Ayisha; Zilla – Mumtasmai; Mabel – Firoze; Quentin – Nared; and Herbert – Sudama. (At a later date, He added: Norina – Noorjehan; and Elizabeth – Dilruba.)

My namesake, Leyla, comes from a Persian story. She was the beloved of Majnun whose intense love and longing for her, although she could not be his, was, after a long time and great suffering, to bring him God-Realization.

Baba loved Italy and particularly Portofino, where He told us He had been before in another advent. He said there were spiritual reasons for our being there and that we would be with Him again in Italy. He added that there were four places in the West of great spiritual significance: Avila in Spain; and Portofino, Venice, and Assisi in Italy. He would often talk about St. Francis of Assisi's love for Christ. He said that we should obey Him and love Him as St. Francis had loved Jesus.

St. Francis had come from a well-to-do Italian family and, after spending a wild youth, he had a vision of Christ which caused him to embrace a life of poverty. He gathered around him a group of disciples which was later to become the Franciscan Order of monks. Despite his poverty, Francis was reported to be "the most joyous of saints" and would have no sad, long faces around him, always rebuking any friar who was gloomy or melancholy. Later in his life, through his intense love for Christ, he received the stigmata (marks of the Cross) and at this time, Baba told us, He also became God-Realized. One of His many legacies was this beautiful prayer:

> Lord make me an instrument of your peace
> Where there is hatred let me sow love
> Where there is injury, pardon
> Where there is doubt, faith
> Where there is despair, hope
> Where there is darkness, light
> Where there is sadness, joy.
>
> O Divine Master, grant that I may not so much seek
> To be consoled, as to console
> To be understood, as to understand
> To be loved, as to love.
>
> For it is by giving that we receive
> It is by pardoning that we are pardoned
> It is by dying that we are born to eternal life.

When we first arrived in Portofino, Baba had told us that He had important spiritual work to do in Italy and He wished to go to Assisi and spend twenty-four hours in a cave that had been used by St. Francis for meditation. On August 1, Herbert was sent in advance to locate such a cave.

Baba, Quentin, Kaka, and Chanji were to follow in five days. The night before they left, while the others were resting, Baba asked us to stay as close to Him as possible. Some of us wandered away and again He asked us to stay close to Him. Suddenly we realized that He was doing special work in advance, as He got that far-away look and His fingers were moving rapidly as if He were setting the seal on work to be done. He seemed to be suffering and was in great pain and we knew something very extraordinary was going to happen but did not know what. Unhappily, some wandered off again only to be sorry later when they found Baba was upset that they could not obey Him in the simplest things.

After some difficulty Herbert was able to find a suitable cave and Baba remained in it alone for nearly twenty-four hours, His companions staying on guard outside to make sure He was not disturbed. On His return to Portofino, Baba still seemed to be suffering, but He was in high spirits and told us about His great meeting in the cave with all the saints and masters of the sixth and seventh planes and how they had mapped out the spiritual destiny of the world for the next two thousand years.

Baba twice went in a rowing boat during our stay at Portofino and we all went on a motor trip to San Fruttuosos which was very exhilarating. But most memorable, perhaps, was a day excursion we took to a mountain near Portofino called Portofino Vetta. A friend of mine, Stephanie Haggard, had arrived to stay for a few days, and Minta and I hired a large carriage drawn by two horses.

Everyone, especially Baba, seemed in a holiday mood that day. We were aware that He was doing great spiritual work all the time, but He also wanted this lighter side and He entered into it as our companion and friend. We had a gramophone and played music as we walked by the carriage, singing and picking flowers from the roadside. There was only one slight mar on the day when, at one point, Baba wanted to stop for lunch, but Quentin said, "No, let's go a little further." This altered Baba's mood for the time being and it was another gentle hint through which He was beginning to show us that obedience to a Master is absolutely necessary. Eventually, we had our picnic lunch at the top of the hill and Baba gave us wine, telling us that when a master gives wine to a disciple, it has great spiritual significance.

During this period, I felt very light hearted; there seemed to be a feeling of living in the eternal moment with Baba, but there were to be many lessons, especially in obedience. One time, as we were walking along the seashore, Baba indicated that He wanted us to go with Him onto a private beach, but Herbert objected and would not come with us. This disobedience meant that Herbert missed seeing an old man with a white beard who took his hat off three times while he looked at Baba. Baba told us later that this old man was a twin in appearance to an agent Herbert would later need to identify in Warsaw.

Herbert also disapproved of our regular visits to Lena's Cafe, where Baba would urge us to eat cakes and ice cream. I don't think Herbert saw such indulgence as the spiritual way to behave, and on top of this Baba would usually ask him to pay the bill. I think this misunderstanding of Baba's way of working was perhaps the beginning of his questioning Baba's methods and why he eventually drifted away.

The boat for India was leaving from Venice and before Baba and the *mandali* embarked, we were allowed to be with Him there for two magical days. We stayed at the International Hotel and Enid Corfe, who had met Baba at East Challacombe and who was working in Italy, joined us there.

We were all stunned with the beauty of Venice, visiting all the well-known sights such as St. Mark's Square, where we listened to the music and had photographs taken feeding the pigeons. One night while we sat there, Baba said, "I am eternally crucified." He seemed so sad and told us that when the burden was very heavy, He sometimes let His disciples share it and gave each as much as they could bear. Then He suddenly got up and made us all walk around St. Mark's.

He told us that Jesus came to Venice before the Crucifixion with two of His disciples and had sat on the exact spot where St. Mark's was built. As we walked someone had to produce a pencil and paper and mark the details as Baba pointed and counted. He explained that the whole structure with its domes and pillars was the exact plan of the inner and outer Circles of the Avatar with the twelve Apostles and the one hundred and eight Outer Circles' members making one hundred and twenty in all. He subsequently gave a new chart for the Circle, but this was the original one He gave in Venice. It was also at Venice that He talked to us for the first time about the Avatar, the first soul in Creation to have gained God-Realization.

We had yet another serious lesson in obedience at the Lido. Baba had asked some of us to go with Him and said that He wanted us to keep near Him and not to stray away sightseeing or shopping. In spite of His repeating this again as an order, some of us drifted away to swim. At this Baba became annoyed. He jumped up and said He wanted to go back. He left for the hotel, followed by Margaret and myself, who were the only two who had stayed with Him. And when Kitty, who had been to Thomas Cook's arranging our tickets returned, she found us in tears.

The rest of the group eventually came back and Baba, in a rather sad mood, said, "The East wants to sit at My feet, but the West wants Me to sit at their feet!" We were all terribly upset to have disobeyed Him and to have been so insensitive to His moods but then, as always, He forgave us.

It was terrible parting from Him this time when He sailed for India, for we had all drawn so much closer to Him in love and He had taught us many needed lessons. He treated us so like children, but He knew that in the future we would need that love He was giving us when we had to come back and face our problems—many of us were to go through a World War. He was feeding us and with each trip there was a little something different which He gave to keep us faithful and steadfast later on when we were hardly to see Him.

At Sea, Piroscafo
22nd Aug. 1932

Dearest Leyla,

Your note was handed to Me by Kaka. It touched Me deeply to read it. I knew it all for a fact how deep were your feelings and how intense your love for Me. You seem to think and feel neglected and sad, but as I already explained to you, it is *not* so. I love you My Leyla, as deeply and as intensely as I love Shalimar or others, and if, for reasons, it is not outwardly expressed, it must not and does not mean otherwise. I know and am so glad to see that you have always been "My faithful one"—always wanting to see Me happy. And whenever I felt sad or in mood, you felt it so keenly and miserably and cried and tried all your best to make Me happy again.... How can I forget it all? I know all, and know all the while how intensely and immensely you love Me, and if you do not know *now* how deep and great My love is for My Leyla, you will one day know it for certain.

Meanwhile, don't at all worry. The feeling of separation is so keen this time I too feel it so much, but the thought of January cheers Me up and I want you to be happy and cheerful at this thought of Me in January. I know you will miss Me terribly.

You tried to express your deep feelings and intense pangs of love by teasing Me, and appearing to be jealous, but I knew how you felt behind it all.

At this period I just existed for Baba's visits and hoped He would take me to be with Him for always. I could not see that He was trying to make me face and understand myself honestly. There should be no escape from life into a pseudo-spirituality—to run away from facing problems and responsibilities. It took time for me to acknowledge honestly to myself that it was partly a desire to escape unsatisfactory conditions that was at the bottom of my wish. I seemed to have built up a false facade of pious morality which Baba was helping to break down, and I already sensed the beginning of a complete reversal of my attitude to life. Time and time again, He has said that one must not divide life into compartments. It must be viewed as a whole and only by going through *Maya* or Illusion can one attain to Reality.

On our return home from Italy, my aunt opened the door to greet Minta and me, and burst into tears. Apparently Mikko, the dog Baba had given me to look after, had been run over shortly after we left. They had thought I would be very upset, but Baba had said to me in Santa Margherita that I should not worry if anything happened to Mikko, so I was prepared for the worst. I knew that Mikko had been used as a symbol or substitute for someone for Baba's work. I was even more sure of this when years later my mother was tragically killed in a road accident in the same way as Mikko. I firmly believe that through Mikko, Baba gave my mother these extra years of life.

Baba had returned to India via Egypt reaching there in September and going straight to Nasik. From Nasik we had many letters:

Nasik
September 9, 1932

Sweetheart Leyla,

I read all your letters every word of which smelled of the sweet fragrance of love running through.

You are not only "faithful" but as your very name indicates "madly in love"—as I alone know. I am now waiting for that happy reunion in January when I will see you with such a delightful outpouring of heart's deep, deep love.

Remember Leyla Mine—none is to worry for Mikko. It was all My work and due to My key.

Give the enclosed to My beloved child Ayisha with best, best love.

M. S. IRANI

Of course, others besides the individual members of Kimco received letters from Baba, including Charles Purdom, the Backetts, and many close ones in America. Baba had asked Charles to write His biography and he was already at work collecting material. This book, called *The Perfect Master*, was eventually published in 1937 and later elaborated into a fuller volume called *The God Man*.

In 1932, the Circle Editorial Committee was set up in London to help spread Baba's message in England with Norina, Herbert,

Kitty, and Will Backett as directors, and Baba, of course, as chairman. Herbert had selected the offices at 50 Charing Cross Road, because they overlooked the Thames and reminded him of one of his favorite quotes from Francis Thompson's *Kingdom of Heaven:* "I see Christ walking on the water, not of Genessereth but Thames." The office was manned mainly by Will, but I used to help. The committee was in operation for many years and was responsible for publishing the booklet *The Sayings of Shri Meher Baba* in 1933 which was the first of its type in the West. Through its work, many people came to find out about Meher Baba, among them Fred Marks and William Donkin. Fred was a prominent member of the British group till his death in 1987 and "Don," who was a well-to-do young medical student, went to stay with Baba in India after he qualified and remained there till his death in 1970.

Kim had been gradually drifting away, but I still saw her as much as I could. I lost track of her completely when she moved to America and she disappeared from the scene for many years. She was to come back later, and I think it would be interesting to quote from a letter she wrote in 1971 about these early days:

> It is difficult to convey the effect Baba had on the early English devotees; sight blotted out, as it were, everything else. I think it was Plato who said to the effect that when the sun shines one doesn't see the stars. We all lived in an enchanted world in which nothing existed save the Beloved....

INVITATION TO INDIA

Happily the reunion with Baba in England took place earlier than we had anticipated:

November 20th, 1932

Dear Kimco,

This is just a hurried report to inform you that Baba is leaving tomorrow by the S.S. CONTE VERDE.

How He has left things here to sail for the West, He alone knows. In spite of all haste and hard—strenuously hard—work till late hours every night ever since He arrived, much of the work is left unfinished. But as He had already promised and wanted to see you, Kimco— His heart—He is leaving here tomorrow—leaving me here to finish His external work, with the help of Adi Senior (Rustom's brother). What the separation from Baba means to me, I can't write.... You, Kimco, need not be told that... but where Baba's work is concerned, personal feelings, however keen or severe, are to be set aside. I had to stay—for His work—to finish it with the aid of Adi, as per His instructions.

All those movements of Baba Himself and His party to the West, and two of us in the East, are for establishing and keeping links (spiritually), as He alone knows, for the great work He has to do. What strain it means to Him, to think of all these, plan and arrange everything to suit all conditions, people, and circumstances, He alone knows.

We (humans) would simply go mad if we merely hear of these. The strain on Him is too hard even to observe, as I already wrote to you. And if the Beloved darling incurs so much of strain on self for the good of humanity, why should we hesitate in doing our bit, however humble or small?

He has left all work at a critical juncture only to come to you and none except He knows what to do next. (And though He has left all instructions to me and Adi to do things in His absence, we don't know what comes next.)

He has cabled you inquiring who of you could come to Egypt to meet Him, if called. I can't understand what He means to do, but He will have to consider *your* case *chiefly* in arranging His plans for the future. So I have no idea what He will do. How He loves you—Kimco— and how He loves Herbert—you know from your heart of hearts. You can imagine for this that He comes to meet you, His heart, leaving His work here unfinished at a critical juncture, and sends Rustom to America via Eastern route to see Herbert besides. He has left me instructions to proceed immediately, when He wires, to China and stay with Herbert awaiting instructions.

It all depends on His future plans and movements whether He proceeds to America or returns to India again. That's why He has sent Rustom to America to stay there till He goes—so that in case His going there is delayed if He returns again to India to finish His work here for a short while, and then go to America, the link would be established and continued through Rustom's presence over there.

Anyhow, He has to go to America as that will be the chief center of His future working, but it's only a question whether He proceeds there *now*—immediately—or a little later. He *might* even take you, Kimco, to India with Him, and oh! what a joy to all of us here to have you with us and to you too—to be in India with Baba—if He does that!

But whatever happens, the thought for the present that He is coming to you, the hopes of a happy reunion soon, will make your very life full of fresh vigor and spirit, to make you the happiest of all!

Wishing you all a glorious treat with Him, with much love from the darling Beloved for you all.

Yours, *Chanji*

We booked rooms for Baba and His party at the Knightsbridge Hotel. Princess Norina Matchabelli and Elizabeth Patterson were there to see Him, so we, the English group, had our first meeting with two of the American group who would be so closely linked with us all in the future.

They had heard of and met Baba through Jean Schloss in New York and already loved Him devotedly and only lived to serve Him. They were both destined to do wonderful work for Him and in those early days their large and varied social, artistic, and business connections were very valuable for His work. Elizabeth was precise and methodical and liked everything to be done well. She was a brilliant businesswoman in the insurance field and, still a devout Christian, would go to church whenever she could. She had an enormous love for animals, especially dogs, and a great sense of humor. Baba would usually team people to work together who had opposite personalities and in Elizabeth's case this was with Norina, but this pairing did have one advantage as Norina would egg Elizabeth on to be a bit more dynamic.

Norina had become famous as Maria Carmi, when she created the role of the Madonna in her first husband's, Karl Volmuller's, play "The Miracle." She was now married to the handsome and popular Prince Matchabelli, and together they made famous Matchabelli perfumes. A strikingly beautiful and volatile woman, Baba said she represented the twelfth of each Circle of the Avatar and was the "changing one" because she changed sex with each advent of the Avatar. He also said if she were present at a gathering then everyone was represented. When I first met her I was a little in awe of her, but later when she was staying in England, at a time when I happened to be a little depressed, she was extremely kind to me and we became great friends.

Norina was very active in bringing old friends to Baba during this visit to London. I think she was secretly a little ashamed of us and felt Baba should meet people of greater social standing. I remember particularly her bringing a Countess Pahlen and

Baroness Rothschild. Both did not stay long, but I do remember that every time Baba was mentioned, Baroness Rothschild would say, "But so Moses said."

We arranged for Baba to have a portrait bust done during this visit by the sculptor, Edward Merrett, which, when finished, we sent to India; but sadly it had somehow been lost. There were also press interviews and many people visiting Baba. Coming to the hotel regularly were of course the Backetts, Charles Purdom, and also the Sharpleys.

Margaret and I were given the task of washing and combing Baba's hair. At that time He had a cloud of hair and after it was washed and combed it stood out round his head in a sort of burnished halo. The first time I had to do it alone, as Margaret had to give a lesson and could not arrive in time. I realized what a great privilege this was, as not many people were allowed to touch Baba's hair, and I was a bit nervous, especially with Kaka clucking around like a mother hen. But I'll never forget how patient Baba was and the childlike pure look on His face. I soon lost my anxiety of pulling or hurting Him and we were all in good humor by the end. After this Margaret and I were automatically hair-washers. And from that time He always referred to me as "the faithful one," but in my heart I felt that this was rather a dull title, and would much rather have been named after some other characteristic He liked.

At this time discussions started about a film that Baba wanted produced about His life. Norina, who was the most qualified because of her connections in the film world, was given the task of organizing it. She approached the film producer Gabriel Pascal, who started work on it. Baba also spoke about His wish to find a special type of boy—"the perfect boy," and, He said, when this boy was found, He would break His silence. Although several candidates were brought to Baba at different times, the perfect boy was never found; but the search occupied a great deal of the time of His disciples in the East and the West over the years, and through it Baba must have been working on the youth of the world and the New Humanity.

He explained that He had three ways of working: individually, collectively through crowds, and universally. By setting each of us different tasks at different times, He worked on us in His own way. He used the technique of change of plans and tension to teach us lessons in obedience; to have poise however demanding the situation; and, of course, fundamentally to have faith in Him.

We little knew we were to have perhaps the greatest of all these tests in the very near future, but at that time we were excited because He had told us that a group of us were to go to India in the spring of the following year, then on to China and Hollywood. Of course, we were wildly excited at the idea, and there were happy discussions to make arrangements; and when Baba left for India via Europe, on December 14, 1932 taking with Him Quentin, Norina, and Elizabeth, He left us with the promise that we would all be joining Him in India soon. He told us we would be with Him forever, and we would get God-Realization when He broke His silence in the Hollywood Bowl.

In Switzerland, He contacted Hedi and Walter Mertens, whose whole family was eventually to follow Baba, and Otto Haas Heye, an art teacher who became devoted to Baba and later came to have a close link with Anita de Caro (now Vieillard). From Europe, Baba returned to India via Egypt and Ceylon, taking Quentin with Him. A letter written to Minta and me from Bandarawala, January 24, 1933:

I have received your cable of 20th, regarding the theater and its worries, three days late owing to the negligence of Cooks. Neither of you must worry. What does money matter when you have Me, the Lord of the World? Leave all to Me, you have not the slightest idea of what happiness lies in store for you!

Leave all future matters to Me, I will arrange everything. I have written all details about your journey to India to Saroja (Kitty), and she will see to your passages.

Darling Shalimar can never be penniless when My love surrounds her, and she knows how much I love her.

What I want you both to definitely understand is that you will both be with Me, wherever I am, whether it is in America, England, or India, and that I want you to do what I instruct you.

I am sending back Nared especially to accompany you all, so that no inconvenience or hitch in your journey may occur.

> All My love,
> beloved ones,
> M. S. IRANI

So Quentin (Nared) was sent back to England and on March 6, 1933, we left from Genoa on the S.S. Victoria with mountains of luggage, confidently expecting to be with Baba forever in India. From England there were Margaret, Mabel, Kitty, Audrey, Minta, Quentin, and myself. There was also a young maid who had waited on Baba in the hotel in London. He had said that she was a very pure type and that when we came to India, Kitty was to arrange for her to come with us. As well as arranging this, Kitty had worked very hard to get us all safely off, paying for the passages of several of us. At Genoa, we were met by Elizabeth, Norina, and a protege of Norina's, Vivienne Giesen. What a strange party we were—one man and so many women.

CHANGE OF PLANS

Thinking that we were leaving England for good, we had given away many of our belongings. Margaret and Mabel had even sold their ballet school. We were loaded with luggage; the plan was for us to accompany Baba through India and China and finally to America where He would break His silence as promised at the Hollywood Bowl. He had told us we would all get God-Realization when He spoke and Norina and Minta had bought special dresses for the occasion. On top of this, Quentin had warned us we might be invited to official functions such as garden parties, so we took formal clothes, hats, and even fur coats. Although we had brought such a quantity of luggage, most of it was destined to stay in store at Thomas Cook's and in any event never left Bombay.

When we arrived at Bombay, there was a reception arranged for us in Kadawali where we met the Eastern women for the first time and found Mehera as beautiful as Baba had described her. It was very gay and animated; as usual Baba was full of fun and we were so very happy to be in India.

In a recent letter, Mehera reminded me: "Just the other day I talked of our meeting in Kadawali and how Baba hid Himself from all of you and we told you that the one who finds Baba will be rewarded with an embrace—you were the lucky one who found Baba."

It was a wonderful experience, traveling with Baba to Kashmir, through the most beautiful scenery in the world with its special spiritual atmosphere. It would seem that perhaps this visit to Kashmir was the real reason for the trip, although we did not realize it at the time. At Agra, Baba started hinting at a change of plans: calling each of us—except Minta—in turn He looked very sad and solemn and asked us to be prepared for any eventuality.

We saw the Taj Mahal, the beautiful memorial built by the Emperor Shah Jehan for his wife, Mumtaz Mai, in daylight and by moonlight which was an unforgettable sight. During the visit Kitty became very agitated, saying she was sure someone was following us. It turned out to be an English reporter who, sensing an unusual story, was already on our trail. Little did we realize what trouble this would lead to in the very near future.

After the stop at Agra, I felt I was in one of those timeless moments with Baba, who looked so beautiful and dynamic at this special time. It was a magical place and a very special privilege to be there with Him although we were feeling bewildered and wondering what was going to happen. We proceeded to Kashmir via Bandadara and Murree, a hill station, most of us frozen by this time as we had left our warm clothing in Bombay, not realizing how cold Kashmir would be.

In Srinagar, we stayed on three house boats on the River Jelum and went on many excursions, including one where Baba pointed out Mount Harvan, where He said Jesus had been buried after the Crucifixion after two of His disciples, Thaddeus and Bartholomew, had brought the body from the Holy Land. But sadly, this wonderful experience of being with Baba in the magnificent country, with the majestic Himalayas in the distance, was almost over. He told us there were spiritual reasons which made it necessary for us to leave India. Though shocked, we all, of course, accepted His decision. In just three weeks we had journeyed from Bombay to Kashmir and back again.

We arrived back in Bombay, after a horrible train journey, exhausted. We did not know it, but Baba had already had our return passages back to Europe booked. So all there was for us to do was to board the boat; we were so numb with shock and exhaustion that we just laid down on our bunks and slept. Margaret was physically sick. But we accepted it as part of our training in detachment and also, of course, in obedience.

Baba had told us He would cable us in Marseilles to tell us what to do, and when we arrived this promised cable was waiting. It instructed Kitty to take charge until Kimco reached England. The others—Norina, Elizabeth, and Quentin—were to stay in Europe. Also waiting for us in Marseilles were reporters wanting interviews for the daily press as there had been widespread publicity about the "Indian Rasputin" that had duped us all. Reading these reports worried my brother so much that he cabled to find out what was happening.

Kitty was in charge of all these interviews in France and again when we arrived back in London, and we were told to keep in the background. Arriving home it was difficult meeting my family; they had been against Minta and me going in the first place, and they now felt very sorry for me and could not understand why I stayed loyal to Baba. I think privately they probably thought it was another of Baba's jokes, like His promises to break His silence.

My mother invited Margaret and Mabel to stay with us until they were able to find a place to live, which was not for long as amazingly, with Baba's guidance, their ballet school came back to them. The person who had taken it over had made such a mess of it that they were able to buy it back and they became more successful than before.

ON THE CLIFF

In June 1933, Baba came to Europe again. Kitty and Minta went in advance to be with Him, first in Spain and then to a villa in Italy, leaving Margaret, Mabel, and me in a terrible state because we were not called. I was particularly jealous that He had taken Minta and not me, as I loved Spain and would have loved to have been there with Him. Then the word came from Baba that Elizabeth had rented another villa, Altachiara in Portofino, for a month and we were to come and join them.

When we got there we met a newcomer, about whom we had already heard a great deal—Anita de Caro. She had been studying acting with Norina. Her reaction when she met Baba for the first time on His visit to Harmon, unlike so many others who wept, was to laugh with joy and she always remained able to amuse Him. She had studied art and painted His portrait on that first visit. At once, she and Minta became great friends, but I did not really come to know her until our later visit to Cannes.

Altachiara was a beautiful place—completely secluded—

with a fine view above the village. As well as those staying there—
Elizabeth, Norina, Herbert, Quentin, Vivienne, Anita, Kitty,
Minta, and myself—there were many visitors: Ruano Bogislav,
Nonny and Rano Gayley, the Mertens with their daughter Anna
Caterina (Baba had great fun with her), Alice and Vicky Traum
from Vienna, and Enid Corfe from Milan. All these disciples now
became part of our daily lives.

Baba seemed very happy in Italy. There was great activity
with discussions about the film and typing of articles and messages.
On a few occasions He again gave us wine for spiritual reasons and
one of my special memories was one moonlit night on the terrace,
with the scent of jasmines wafting to us and the sound of the
cicadas, Baba lying in a royal blue jacket with His hair like a halo
around His glowing face. He looked so very beautiful as we all sat in
silence enfolded in His love.

Of course there were upheavals as always with Baba. Altachiara was haunted and we complained about having our hair pulled
and being pushed out of bed. Baba said that the ghosts were
pleading with Him to release them and it culminated one night
when I thought I saw one of the ghosts and screamed. In fact, it
turned out to be Margaret out for an evening stroll. In the uproar
that followed, there was a knock at the bedroom door. It was Kaka
sent by Baba to see what all the commotion was about. The next
morning Baba came while we were having breakfast and said there
was one quality He admired in His Western followers and that was
their courage. But He also told us that that night He had given the
unhappy ghosts their freedom.

Later there was more trouble. Baba said we were always
quarreling and did not realize what it meant to be with a Master.
He announced He was cutting short His stay and leaving. Of

course we were devastated and all wept; I can still see Elizabeth weeping copiously into a large serviette. Eventually, of course, He forgave us and stayed.

Again, as on our previous visit, we frequently went to Lena's Cafe for ice cream and cakes. And then Baba decided to go to Rome for a few days taking with Him Norina, Herbert, Elizabeth, Minta, and Kitty. Those of us left behind were told to arrange an entertainment for His return.

We evolved several sketches and dances: Margaret and Quentin did a skit on Meredith and Margaret Starr; Mabel played an African chieftain with Anita and myself as native women; and it ended with a combined sketch, Margaret playing Norina, and Mabel, Anita, and myself as old, old women, knitting and still hopefully saying that we believed the perfect boy would be found and Baba would speak. Margaret, as Norina, came in to say that the boy had been found but then Quentin, playing Kaka, came in with a cable saying that due to the eruption of Vesuvius everything has been postponed. We all fainted, saying, "We still have faith!" When we performed it for Baba He was greatly amused. He never took offense at such sketches and afterward we all enjoyed a buffet supper with Him.

A major episode at this time was a dangerous incident that happened one day when Baba and a crowd of us started out for a walk along the cliffs. Most of us had wandered back to the villa by the time the party came to a dangerous ravine down to the sea. There were only two men and two girls still with Baba as He led them back by another route. Then they came up against a sheer rock face which Baba, being more agile, was able to climb, mounting higher and higher on the cliffs while the others were left struggling. At one point they could go no further and were in danger of falling down a sheer drop into the sea. Baba, now at the top of the cliff, clapped His hands for help and was heard by one of the Italian boys who went to bring a rope. A rescue party arrived and by means of the rope was able to pull the others to safety.

When He returned to the villa, Baba seemed quite happy and He explained that He used the energy, courage, and emotion released in this incident for His spiritual work. He gave us all wine to celebrate the happy outcome of what had really been a dangerous situation, which I think Jean summed up very well in her book, *Avatar*:

> In psychological terminology this adventure suggests an important step taken in consciousness perhaps by the four who participated in it, perhaps by four types or sections of humanity whom these men and women represented. With the help of the spiritual guide they made their descent to the realm of the unconscious— the sea—in safety; but their return journey to balanced integrated consciousness was fraught with hazards and danger spots. The guide, being sure-footed and nimble, as the awakened higher consciousness always is, ascended quickly and easily to the safety of Mother Earth. Having drawn them up into the safety of his own plane the Master Guide shared with them the wine, symbol of the redeemed life.

There is a postscript to this cliff story. Some time ago, some Baba lovers visiting Portofino met a local ferryman who, amazed to see Baba's picture on buttons on their jackets, kept saying, "He is the Baba!" Delighted to discover that he knew of Baba, through a halting conversation they found out that when he was a little boy "the Baba," who did not speak, had come to Portofino. The ferryman was very proud of the fact that during the cliff drama it was he alone who understood that Baba's gestures meant that He wanted a rope. Not only that, but his family owned Lena's Cafe where our group so often had refreshments. He was delighted to take them in his boat to the cafe where his family still lived. There they met his mother who was ill in bed. Her room was full of pictures of Christ and the saints and there was a little altar with Christ's photo inside. She remembered Baba and the group well and her son explained to her that "the Baba" was now loved and followed all over the world.

Baba sailed for Bombay on July 24, 1933. Kitty had been sent back to London in advance of the rest of us to find a house where we could all live until He returned. She found one in Ealing, West London, and we all moved in. I was told I could go home for weekends and Minta and Christine could come when they wished. Herbert had returned from abroad but he had started to wobble in his loyalty to Baba although Kitty took no notice. She never swerved once from her belief in Baba—her love was like a rock. Charles Purdom was still working on his book and he asked us all to send any notes we had that might help him. The rest of our time we spent devising an entertainment for Baba in His next visit.

This was on October 9, 1933, when He stayed at a vegetarian hotel, Hygeia House. I booked a room there too, so I could be on hand to do any secretarial work and to receive and show people in and out. It was there that Quentin brought the famous actor-manager Ivor Novello to see Baba and when he had left, Baba said, "He is my man." Ivor invited Baba to see his current play and put a box and several stalls at His disposal. After the show he came round, embraced Baba and introduced Him to Zena and Phyllis Dare, two musical comedy actresses, and invited Him to stay at his home whenever He wished.

My brother Jack, manager and writer, had kindly lent us the "Q" Theatre to stage the show we had devised at Ealing and he also helped us at the dress rehearsal with lighting and production and use of staff. As a result, this was the best and most professional show we ever did for Baba. It was performed before an invited audience and Baba seemed to enjoy it very much. There were many short sketches and recitations including Vivienne, dressed a la Isadora Duncan, dancing a solo to my recitation of "The Blessed Damozel," Anita and I dressed as angels. Minta danced a rumba with Quentin who also did a scene from *The Taming of the Shrew*. Mabel did several really funny numbers; and a hunting scene, performed to the music of "Do You Ken, John Peel," with Margaret as the fox, Quentin the hunter, and Anita and I as the hounds, lying on our backs and waving our legs and arms in the air, brought the house down.

One day we all went down in a bus to visit Will and Mary in their home near Sevenoaks. They gave us a warm welcome and somehow Mary managed to make tea for all of us. It was a most happy day, especially for "Wilmar" to have Baba there to sanctify their little home.

Baba left for Spain on December 22, 1933, taking with Him Minta, Kitty, Norina, Elizabeth, Quentin, and the *mandali*. They were lucky enough to go on to Marseilles and see Baba off on the Viceroy of India. Enid Corfe and Otto from Zurich were also there.

At sea November 12, 1933, Baba wrote to me:

We arrive Bombay early morning 14th. The voyage,

though comfortable, was rather boring, as I missed the love and company of My dearest.

I know how you have been feeling and missed your beloved darling. But this is all going to end now, after six months. Rest assured.

I want you and all to give serious attention to the film work I have allotted to each of you, and not to feel sad or dejected. You know how I love you, and want you to be always happy, and love you to be with Me, but for the great work that lies ahead, all must put up with some pains. Our happy reunion after six months will be all the more sweet for the separation you now feel and suffer for Me. I know it. So, My dearest Leyla, be a good darling and in the thoughts of a happy reunion after six months, and of the great work you have to do for your beloved B., be happy and keep cheerful. There is no need now to tell you I am always with you for *I* AM with you always, as you are with Me, forever and ever. You know that.

My unbounded love, and loving go with this for My beloved Leyla.

Ever yours,
M. S. IRANI

Try to get a bit fat and strong.

If I don't write for the first fortnight in India due to pressure of work, don't you worry... I will be writing separately after 15 days.

A DIVINE ART

 Baba arrived back in India November 14, and went to Nasik and then Meherabad. To cheer us up He had told us, before He left, that we were all to play leading roles in the film Pascal was producing—imagine how excited we all were. While He was away, from November 1933 to June 1934, to give myself an insight into film production, I became involved with film work, through my agent brother, Herbert. I was able to do some crowd work which I found tiring but interesting.

In Baba's absence, Margaret, Mabel, and I kept in touch and saw each other frequently, sharing the letters we received from Baba.

Nasik
November 20, 1933

My dear Leyla,

As I wrote you from the boat I miss you very, very much all the time, and though I am the course of all Life and Love, I *do* long for our happy reunion after six months—and they *will* pass quickly My darling. Till then try your best to carry out My instructions to the letter, and not worry. I know perfectly how you feel and how you are pining to be with Me again. But this time we shall be together for long, so try to be cheerful— don't be depressed, for My sake.

We reached Bombay on the 14th morning instead of the 13th as we were delayed a few hours in the Suez Canal. Many of My devotees came to receive Me—I stayed the morning in Bombay and then motored to Nasik. You can imagine how terribly happy the Gopies and everybody else were to have Me back.

All My disciples here are delighted about the film and are eagerly looking forward to start work. Preparations are going on—Elizabeth is sending the equipment soon, so I will be busy supervising the work, but you know that I am with you all the time, and you are always in My heart.

With all My love.

> My darling Leyla,
> M. S. *IRANI*

P. S. I got your letter this morning. Don't be disappointed My darling Leyla, and don't be depressed if you can't get work, go on trying, I'll help you. If you don't get parts, concentrate on studying acting—be cheerful—six months will pass quickly.

Baba would often call His women disciples His "Gopies," which were the milkmaid companions of Krishna from Hindu legend. Not having been lucky enough to go to Spain with Baba, Margaret, Mabel, Quentin, and I now took a holiday there and followed in His footsteps to Madrid and Avilla.

Meherabad
Ahmednagar
December 18, 1933

Darling Leyla,

I have all your letters, narrating interesting experiences of your visit to Spain, how you followed My path from London to Paris, Madrid, Barcelona, Marseilles, and back, and the beautiful contacts you found and formed. It was good work indeed to bring other dear ones to My love and devotion, and it is quite probable some, if not all, will see Me and be of use one time or another in future.

RE: playing parts in "Q," try to make the most of the chances you get. Yes, you are quite right. Try to sublimate all your feelings for love and never mind the changes. Try to adjust yourself to these, and you will get your chance to do creative work, as you desire.

So you have arranged a Xmas party. Well, we shall meet there for I shall *have to be* there to meet My dear ones.

All My love,
M. S. *IRANI*

This was a period when I was feeling rather isolated and depressed, and, of course, as usual Baba always attacks your weaknesses. He condemned depression particularly, telling us on one occasion how important it was to always look cheerful, for it was, He said, "A Divine Art."

> Meherabad
> Ahmednagar
> January 10, 1934

My ever faithful Leyla,

...would you, darling, give up that look and air of depression, and be more cheerful, gay, and happy? I love you so to look and be always happy. Clouds of depression may come and go, but there is always the sun of happiness behind them. Don't you know, Leyla dearest, how I love you to be with Me always, and am actually working here for the same—to bring about the happy reunion which is ever your delight and dream. But, in the meantime, go on with your work. Things will ease gradually. But when they look complicated, don't despair. I know how you feel the separation—how all else is lifeless to you without Me, but don't you My dearest. That time too is coming when you will be with Me, work with Me, for Me and My cause. Let Me arrange things as I want, and only do as I say. I know you always try your best, but I also know that you at times worry, which I don't want you to do. Time does hang heavy when separation is keenly felt, but remember "even this shall pass away." You are one of My nearest and dearest who are always in My thoughts wherever I am, wherever you are and each of you have a great part to play in the great work that is ahead, and for which I am preparing you. So again I say, darling Leyla, don't worry.

> Always with you,
> With all My love,
> M. S. IRANI

At this time I had become a vegetarian (Baba sometimes told people not to eat meat but He did not make it a general rule), which worried my mother so much she wrote to Baba.

> Meherabad
> Ahmednagar
> February 14, 1934

My ever faithful Leyla,
 I received all your letters. Also one from your dear mother—she is such a dear. I love her because she loves you both so much and wants you to be happy and healthy, as I want you to be. She can't bear "to see you—her own child—growing so thin and weak, and frail." I understand that, and really do feel for her. I see nothing wrong if you eat meat—not much—*but twice a week* only and in *small quantities*—until further instructions. I understand you wish to obey My orders *implicitly* whatever happens, and I am glad you did up till now, so unflinchingly, irrespective of any considerations of your health. A faithful "Leyla" only could do that. I love you so—and lovingly and willingly tell you this—to be taking meat twice a week, without *worrying* or thinking of anything else. It will please your dear

mummy so, which will please Me. For I love the dear old soul, for all the love she has for you two, My dearest gopies. So, once again, I tell you, don't think any more about this and do as I say. And, under no circumstances be cross with your dear mother. It is *My Wish* that you *don't say anything to her*—not even about her writing to Me. Go on as if you don't know anything, and say you have My orders to eat meat twice a week. I am writing her that way.

Leyla has no thought but of her beloved Majnun—so have you—of none else but of your beloved darling, whom you adore. And you need not be told that your Beloved loves you and that you are always in his thoughts—though not always externally expressed. It is because of an inner assurance that I do feel from such "faithful" ones like you, who would never fail in their love, that I work here so freely, without any worries from you. Bravo, darling Leyla. Cheer up dearest. Perhaps the happy reunion you have been dreaming of may be very soon, and even if postponed, have you not that steadfastness and strength of faith and depth of love that could keep you up till then? You have that, I know. But I won't leave you dearest ones, any longer. You know that, so be happy, cheerful, and singing songs of a happy reunion, to bring it nearer with all the force of your soul, I want to be amused with these.

All My love,
M. S. *IRANI*

This letter shows Baba's amazing kindness and exquisite consideration for the feelings of other people. I am always amazed that Baba gave us so much of His time and showered so much love on us. Many times I felt so unworthy and felt that I failed Him so often, and I know others felt the same way.

> Meherabad
> Ahmednagar
> February 28, 1934

My darling Leyla,

I received your letters... the bust has arrived. I am so glad you encouraged the sculptor who did it for Me. My darling gopies know what I would like.

And what makes you say you are such "poor lot of disciples?" Have you no love? And if you have "love" you have everything. There is nothing to compare with "love." And I know how much "love" you have for Me.

I am glad to know about My birthday party of My own dearest ones. And I received your so many xxxxxxx specially sent that day.

> All My love,
> My ever faithful Leyla,
> *M. S. IRANI*

The bust referred to by Baba and a bronze hand we also sent were mislaid in India, although several of us were given plaster copies of the hand by Baba.

Mysore
March 16, 1934

Darling Leyla,

I have all your letters and the loving birthday message and need I tell you ever faithful Leyla how happy all your letters make Me. Leyla knows her Lord (Majnun) much better for words.

And you ask Me, "What am I doing?" My dearest, if you only knew...! But you will, pretty soon. And it is such a big "surprise!" You will dance for joy as you never before have. You couldn't have dreamt of such a surprise that will amply recompense for all the anxiety you have had during this long spell of silence that has been such a test, I know. The admirable patience you and the other dearest ones have kept is not unknown to your beloved, who had all this while planned "something" for his loved ones that will really surprise all beyond imagination! Just wait a little, and you will know it.

And don't let things worry you darling. Take it all easy and keep cheerful. For, are you not Mine, and being Mine, you must be brave—as brave as you are faithful.

RE: *East Challacombe*—I do love your efforts and anxiety to do something for the work, but dearest, it is not the thing required and hence I didn't wire. I am planning "something" very surprising for you all dearest.

I read what you wrote about your dear old grandmother. Yes, I am with her.

It has been a long spell of silence indeed, but it had its great purpose, as explained in My general letter, and I am happy for you all, My dearest, for this great test you have passed through and that has really brought you all so closer, as you could hardly ever imagine. But you will know.

Give My love to all the dearest ones of the group and to others who need, except to My dearest Leyla, to whom I give it Myself with a hearty embrace and a thousand loving xxxxxx.

M. S. IRANI

East Challacombe was for sale and I had thought I might buy it and make it a permanent center for Baba. But obviously Baba did not want it at that time.

Meherabad
April 14, 1934

My ever faithful darling Leyla,

I have all your letters, the last enquiring about going to Spain, and about learning shorthand. Yes, dearest, you can go to Spain, and also study shorthand. In short, I want you to be busy and in any way keep yourself cheerful and happy under all conditions.

Yes, the great moment is now approaching, and this last intervening period is one of suffering, for Me and also for those who are Mine. And whenever you have to face things and facts that pain and puzzle you, remember you are Mine. That will enable you to stand anything boldly and cheerfully. I know you will, with all your heart, for you are My ever faithful and beloved Leyla.

I am busy arranging things prior to My retirement, but anyway remember, I want you to be writing to Me wherever I am, even on the Himalayas, for I shall be in touch with you My dearest gopies even through correspondence, although as a matter of fact, I am always with you in spirit. Distance in space and delays in correspondence do not matter where love binds the dearest ones in a bond that is ever inseparable! And you, My ever dearest Leyla, are so close at heart and so constant in My thoughts too.

The film work, as reported from the other end, is progressing gradually.

All My love—Remember dearest I am always with you and you belong to Me, forever.

M. S. IRANI

In so many of these letters it can be seen that Baba tried and tried again to hammer at my many weaknesses by the device of reiteration. The most difficult thing for me was not to worry. Baba has told us not to worry as it is a serious dissipation of psychic energy. Gradually, as I tried, I did change and became more lighthearted though. Of course, there are always battles to be fought, for the ego is hydra-headed and it is so easy to deceive yourself. In the course of the years I have observed, in myself and others, how Baba has helped us to break down many of our rigid preconceptions.

LETTER TO MINTA

When Baba came to England again on June 24, 1934, I had a flat in Hampstead all ready for Him to stay. It was a large flat with a garden, lent by my sister-in-law, and so we were able to accommodate Baba, Elizabeth, Norina, Kitty, Margaret, Mabel, and myself. The men *mandali* and Quentin stayed at Margaret's flat not far away.

My mother was then staying with my aunt and grandmother at the Star and Garter Hotel in Richmond (now the Petersham Hotel). Baba promised to see her so Minta drove us over and He had tea with them in their private sitting room overlooking the river. He was so kind and gentle with the old people and we naively accepted all this, not properly realizing how amazing it was that the Lord of the Universe, in the midst of all His work and activities, should find the time to visit one's relations.

Although, as always, He was attentive and charming, at one time He got a far-away look in His eyes and went out and stood quite a while alone on the balcony, looking at the river and the whole panorama, which is a very famous view. It was to this area that, in the 1960s, a group of young Baba lovers came to live and work.

After ten days of great activity—discussing the film and receiving many visitors—Baba left for Zurich to stay at the Mertens' house again, and Kitty, Minta, Norina, Elizabeth, Quentin, and I accompanied Him. How they found room for all of us was incredible: apart from Baba, the *mandali*, and us, there was Anita, who was living there; and staying in the village were Ruano, Nonny and Rano Gayley, Rosmond Wise (a painter friend of Anita's), and Gabriel Pascal.

Pascal had a very strong personality and was very enthusiastic and dynamic. He was not happy with the way the film was going and had come to tell Baba that it was wasting his time. He also planned, at this his first meeting, to trap Baba with questions, but he was completely overcome and fell at His feet: "I was at once His devoted servant!"

I went through another crisis similar to Lugano, thinking that I was being neglected in favor of others, as Baba had told everyone they would go with Him to America where the film was being produced, but had left me out. I thought Baba was going to leave me behind which made me miserable enough, but to cap it all I was stung by a horsefly and became quite disfigured by a swollen eye. I shall never forget how sweet Norina was to me, enfolding me in her arms and whispering that it would be all right.

Sure enough, at my last interview with Baba, He tapped His pocket and said, "If I have to put you in my pocket I will take you with me." At once, my swollen eye, symbol of my inner turmoil, went down. Of course, I now realize that this was a test to see how I would take not being with Baba.

During this time Baba spent one day on the mountain,

Fallenfluh, near Schwyz, in the heart of Switzerland. He did important spiritual work here. Accompanied only by Kaka—no one else was allowed near. He sat in a hollow where He held a meeting with the advanced souls of Switzerland. He drew a circle around Switzerland so that it would not become involved in the Second World War. Indeed, after the war, a German general told Irene Billo that he could not understand why the Germans were unable to penetrate Switzerland!

Baba was returning to India, and as Quentin and I were planning to meet Margaret and Mabel for a second holiday in Spain, He let us travel with Him to Marseilles along with Norina and Elizabeth. The Gayleys were also with us, and one day when we were in a taxi together, I remember Baba smiling and looking at Nonny and spelling out on the board the word "Angel!"

At this time Quentin started to drift away from Baba. He still loved Him but he seemed to find the unquestioning obedience Baba demanded very hard. Baba had asked Quentin and me to buy some birds in a little cage. Nonny then bought a beautiful big cage and Baba asked Quentin to transfer the birds from the original cage to the new one. Quentin was making tea—a task he took very seriously—and did not do it immediately. Baba called a second time and Quentin gave the same reply, that he was busy making tea. In the end, Baba's youngest brother, Adi, changed the birds over and in the process one of the birds flew away. Baba was very angry and said that no one in India would have dared to disobey Him in this way.

Baba often worked with animals, especially dogs and birds. Each one He worked with would get a spiritual push, but at such times He must have been also working on another level. He told us later this same drama took place in the time of Buddha, and it shows how important it is to obey Baba instantly and without equivocation. It was the second time to my knowledge that Quentin's disobedience had made Baba angry—the first being when Baba gave us wine at Zurich and offered to give Quentin some more which he refused.

The next day Baba asked Quentin and me to buy as many birds as we could, eventually taking thirty-two to India with Him when He sailed from Marseilles on July 30, 1934.

> Meherabad
> Ahmednagar
> August 23, 1934

My darling Leyla,

Just had your letter from Spain, and am glad to know you like your lodging in Spain.

The company of the dear gopies will compensate, in a way, for the separation you feel for your Beloved Baba.

The love of Leyla has made history, and is proverbial because of its purity, depth, and intensity. And aren't you the beloved Leyla of your dearest Baba? And what else matters where love such as yours exists? So, My darling, and ever faithful Leyla, why worry?

The birds have all arrived safe, and all here are so glad to have them.

> Ever yours,
> with all My love,
> *M. S. IRANI*

We were not to see Baba again till November 30, four months

later, when He stayed again at Hygeia House, this time for only six days. London was celebrating the wedding of the Duke and Duchess of Kent and was full of people; and Baba, who liked to work with crowds, drove through the streets and mingled with the happy people. Our little group was with Him constantly and on this visit many new people came to see Him. But as His main work was in America, He left for His third visit there on December 5.

Minta was in New York and Baba saw her and arranged for her to go to Hollywood with Him. She said she was very happy in that period but, in fact, it was to be the last time she was to be with Baba.

She wrote to me:

> We used to go for lovely walks every afternoon and return as the sun set. I didn't have much time alone with Baba, He was so busy, but He was very sweet to me. Nonny was specially sweet to me. I shared a bedroom with Rano. There was a lovely Mimosa tree in front of the villa.

I've heard Adi Sr. tell the story that he got Kaka to ask Minta for some chocolates. Of course, such actions without Baba's sanctions were forbidden, and eventually Minta, feeling guilty, confessed to Baba. Kaka was blamed until Adi owned up, but all were severely reprimanded.

Also there were Elizabeth, Norina, Jean and Malcolm, and Ruano Bogislav, a masculine lady who smoked cigars and who Baba called His "eagle" because of the gestures she made. She had a very testing time being put to do all the chores. But, as Jean summed it up: "For three wonderful weeks we were recharged by His radiant presence."

On January 18, 1935, Baba left Hollywood for India and when He arrived back He started arrangements for a period of seclusion, and the Rahuri Ashram for the mad and *masts* (God-intoxicated souls) was started at this time. A letter from Mount Abu, July 25, 1935:

> My darling Leyla,
>
> I have all your loving letters giving news of yourself and also of things and affairs at your end—re your going to Spain and about Minta and other dear ones coming into your contact.
>
> You say you are all scattered about in different places, and feel concerned! Why, dearest? Anything that keeps one busy anywhere must be welcome. My *mandali* here are scattered too, and I am Myself away and aloof from all, on these mountains. And there is a purpose, dearest, behind everything, especially behind all I do, for My circle, *mandali*, and others in general. It may make one look scared, at times, but later on when the outcome is seen or experienced and the object behind all this is revealed, all do understand. But all must wait for that. You will know, one day, everything. Meanwhile, just follow your right impulse wherein you will always be guided and helped by your beloved who looks after you as you can scarcely imagine! So, darling, go to Spain, spend your time in good work, keep cheerful all the while, and return when you feel your work there is finished, or before if you are needed elsewhere and informed. In short, dearest, learn to accept things

as they come, quietly, without worrying and much of the anxiety that is unnecessary will disappear, and things will look easier than at first.

Yes, I might come by the end of the year if I see the necessity, and after finishing the picture, retire there for the rest of the period. For the present, I must be in seclusion and work. And if letters take longer than usual, it will be due to the importance of the work in hand, and should not be taken for anything else. You should never think that I love you the less for that, and should go on writing yourself, as you have been doing up till now, giving news about yourself and the dear ones of the group.

And you are reading the life of Ramakrishna and Vivekananda and you think you like them better than Baba. But whether you like one or the other, it is all Baba. So even if you like Ramakrishna better, it makes no difference, for in Ramakrishna, too, I was; rather, I was he. But I know that Leyla, anyway, won't falter in her love. At least *My Leyla* won't.

And why think of grey hair and getting old and haggard? Does Love grow less for look and age? Why, it grows all the more ripe, intense, and deeper with age and experience. So, dearest, why worry about looks? Whatever you are—withered, shattered, weather-beaten, wishy-washy, pulled-down, or whatever you look, frail, fragile, flimsy, rickety, drooping, tottering, and so on and so on—you will ever be the same "loving and lovely" Leyla in the eyes of your beloved, who looks to no outward form or appearance but to the inner being, the beauty of the heart, the depth of the soul. And besides, I know that whenever I come, you dearest look lovelier, fresher, livelier than ever, in the ecstasy of seeing and being with your beloved, whose dearest darling you are. Convey My love, as ever, to dear Kim, to your dear mother, and also to all the dear ones of the group, and to others who need and seek, in Spain.

All My love,

M. S. IRANI

Then at last we knew the result of Baba's plans for us. He arrived in England on November 3, 1935, to arrange for the American and English group to go back with Him to India where a new ashram at Nasik had been made ready for them. He stayed again at Hygeia House. John Bass, who was not to come to India, and Jean and Malcolm came over from America to see Him there. Jean and Malcolm left for India in advance and Norina, Elizabeth, Nonny, and Rano joined them at Marseilles. Garret Fort and Nadine Tolstoy came together from the U.S.A. and Ruano arrived later, via the Pacific.

Baba said we would all stay for five years, no matter what, and we were all asked to state that we were prepared to stay for that time. We went with this intention, loaded with luggage. Minta was supposed to join us with her daughter Pat but she changed her mind and wrote Baba to this effect.

My sister Minta, "Shalimar" as Baba called her, loved Baba and never turned against Him, but she did not seem able to obey Him in the way He demanded. In 1940 He wrote her this very compassionate letter and she did see Him again, for the last time, in 1956.

Dearest Shalimar,

Your last letter "ticked Me off" for tampering or balancing My Eternal Suffering with Eternal Bliss, whilst humanity has to suffer without joy or Infinite Bliss and happiness, implying was it fair?

Darling Shalimar—I want you to be always outspoken and free with your Beloved. I know you love, but imperfectly as yet, hence your lack of understanding. The Avatar has to suffer eternally for the world, but added to this is the often unnecessary suffering caused by his dearest and chosen ones just because they do not understand Him or His ways.

This gift of understanding is more precious than any other attribute of Love—be it expressed in service or sacrifice. Love can be blind, selfish, greedy, ignorant, but love with understanding can be none of these things. It is the Divine fruit of Pure Love, the rare fruit or flower of the Universe. It has been called "The Sweetest Flower in all the world!" Age cannot wither it. It grows more lovely as it casts off its outer garment, disclosing its unseen beauty within.

What a wonderful opportunity to learn this "Love and Understanding" is given to those whom the Beloved—Himself the epitome of "Perfect Understanding"—calls to live near Him and what a tragedy for those who refuse. If they had any understanding of what they had "passed over" their suffering would indeed be unbearable. No physical suffering, no suffering of the present war could compare with it. Had they had understanding they never would have refused.

How complicated is Life!

You criticize; you take lightly what should be taken seriously. You long at times to please Me, but you don't know how to and you refuse to be taught. You will sacrifice home, child, money, and freedom to understand and learn the art of the theater, the genius of the poet or painter in the pursuit of happiness. You spare no pains to try to understand what interests you, but when I, your Beloved, say "Learn of Me" and "Perfect Understanding, the fruit of Pure Love," you are not prepared to sacrifice anything for its possession. What sort of love is this, I ask? Love cannot force. To serve, please, and love Me is a very different thing from what, let us say, Hitler asks of his followers. They obey—if not they are shot or imprisoned. My followers obey Me voluntarily—a far more difficult ideal.

Learn eventually you will, but in a school where suffering may not be combined with the presence of eternal bliss and happiness as it would if you had come to Me as I asked. There is so much in you which I need for My work. Such capacity to understand, had you the desire to learn and the grit, determination, and courage to strive for the goal. Who better than you were able to realize My changing moods, My present need, My unspoken wish; but you grew tired and wanted change! Like a child, you wanted the fairy palace, the fine jewel, without the climb and toil for its attainment.

No, darling Shalimar, don't be miserable because this time I have "ticked you off!" Write again soon and tell Me all your plans and what you would like to do. You have chosen the longer of two Paths toward the happiness you sincerely desire, but *it is a path* and I will lead you along it to the end. So you have nothing to fear, nothing to worry about. Mine you always were and Mine you will always remain whether there or here.

All My love to dearest Shalimar and a kiss to Pat.

M. S. IRANI

HARD NUTS TO CRACK

Nasik was a wonderful period for all of us. It was the first time we from the West were invited to go and live and work with the Eastern disciples. During the five years we were to be there, Baba said He wanted to train us in discipleship. He added that we were hard nuts to crack but He intended to crack us.

When we left for India, there had been a rumor that King Edward was about to abdicate if he were not allowed to marry Mrs. Simpson; and Kitty, Margaret, and I heard the abdication broadcast when we were aboard the English ship at Marseilles. When we saw Baba we asked Him about it. He said Edward had done the right thing and would come to love Him one day as we did. Meaning, I suppose, that sacrifice and intense love for another could lead to spiritual enlightenment. It was one of the great love stories of history.

The English group, consisting of the Backetts, Tom Sharpley, Margaret, Kitty, and myself arrived on Christmas Eve—the others, except Sam Cohen who arrived a few weeks later from

America, were already there. This was the first Christmas we had spent with Baba. We handed in the various presents we had brought and in the evening, at a real Christmas feast, Baba distributed these Himself and Kaka made a speech which amused us, as all we could really understand was that he kept saying, in his broken English, "No discuss!"

Nasik, sited on holy River Godvari, is one of the sacred cities of India, dedicated to Ram and Sita. Baba's ashram was on land belonging to Rustom Irani whose wife Dolly stayed in the main bungalow with Norina, Rano, Elizabeth, and Nonny, while the rest of us lived in a lovely bungalow that had been specially built for us. There were two of us to a room—I shared with Margaret—and we shared a little shower room with the next room. We each had a wardrobe and dressing table—all of which was comparative luxury compared to the conditions experienced by the Westerners who were to stay at Meherabad later on.

At this time Baba had two other centers besides Nasik: Meherabad, where the women *mandali* lived; and Rahuri, the "mad" ashram where the mad and *masts* were housed. Baba divided His time between these centers, spending three days a week with us at Nasik.

This visit too proved to be, on a superficial level, a time of stress and upheaval. Each one of us was given a task and some of us two; I was made head gardener, with Ruano as my assistant, although ironically she was an expert gardener and I didn't know the first thing about it! This, of course, was the cause of much friction; like the time I rooted up a priceless tree as I had been told that it attracted snakes. But, strangely enough, although I was afraid of snakes, I did not see one the whole time I was in India, while others did.

Ruano also had to look after the birds which Baba had taken back from Marseilles although many of them had died. I picked flowers daily from the garden, and Mary made beautiful arrangements with them. It was Will and Mary's first experience of living in an ashram in this relationship with Baba, but poor Will was ill most of the time and spent a great deal of it in bed. Malcolm and Garret were busy with plans for starting a magazine called, the *Meher Baba Journal.* Unfortunately this partnership led to a break-up between Malcolm and Garret. Jean was also drawn into the argument and it eventually led to Garret being sent back to America. I had always found him a most generous man but he seemed to fit into ashram life even less than the rest of us.

As a result, the *Meher Baba Journal* did not come into existence until after our return from Cannes a year later, when Elizabeth took over as editor. Norina suggested that there should be a discourse by Baba in each issue and these messages from Baba, written down by Dr. C. D. Deshmukh, were later published as *Discourses.*

Perhaps Rano and Margaret had the best jobs. Rano was painting marvelous paintings under Baba's direction and Margaret was given the task of choreographing dances to themes Baba gave her and which He said would be used in the film when it was made. I was lucky enough to be present when she showed Baba what she had created: one, I remember, was called "The Dance of the Mirrors" and another was a Spanish dance. She also had to give Rano and me a daily dancing lesson and at the end of the time we had to perform a hornpipe for Baba, with poor Kitty banging away on the piano. In addition, all of us were given Hindustani lessons by Ramjoo—I must confess we were hopeless.

Along with these special tasks allocated to each one by Baba, we had a daily meditation hour, which pleased the Americans but not us so much. So Baba told Kitty, Margaret, and me that we need not meditate but should just sit and think of Him. He came to call Kitty, Margaret, and me "The Frivolous Three" because we liked parties, but He added, "Be gay, but not frivolous."

We were allowed to go on excursions which tended to start very early in the morning, especially our weekly visit to Meherabad when we set off at midnight in order to avoid the heat of the day. Mehera, Mani, and the women were at Meherabad and for Margaret, Kitty, and me who had met them in 1933, it was a particular joy to renew our acquaintance. We went several times to the house on Meherabad Hill and on one occasion they dressed us all in saris and we had photos taken with Baba. Mani would often arrange entertainments for us; this was the first time we became familiar with her considerable theatrical talents. On one day we went for a picnic, and finally we were allowed to sleep at Meherabad for one night.

We were also taken to Rahuri to see the mad and *masts* and on seeing us, one *mast* asked Baba, "Who are those mad people?" Baba explained that when He washed the mad at Rahuri, He was washing universally and that phase of humanity would benefit just as when He washed the poor and lepers elsewhere.

We went on trips to Trimback, the Pandeluna Caves, and to Happy Valley, which Ram and Sita are said to have visited during their exile and which is close to the place which in later years was to become Baba's home, Meherazad. On the day we visited Happy Valley, Rustom was with us and this turned out to be the last time we saw him because he disappeared shortly afterward.

At Nasik we would sit in the garden round Baba, and I remember one evening in the moonlight when we were all in complete silence; everything was alive with His love and His face had that same radiance I had noticed that evening in Altachiara. This was a special type of *sahavas*. After all, Baba has said that things that are real are given and received in silence.

The highlight of our stay was to be Baba's forty-second birthday celebrations in February. Baba was fasting for forty days beforehand and in turns we were allowed to share this fast with Him. In spite of this fast Baba was supervising every detail of the arrangements for the celebration. A large tent was being erected on the grounds and ten thousand lepers and beggars were to be brought for Baba's *darshan*.

On anyone's birthday we were allowed to have ice cream and it happened that Baba was there for mine on February 10. We had put on our best dresses as we always did when Baba was coming and were ready to go into the dining room when a message came summoning Margaret and me to Baba. I went quite happily expecting a special birthday greeting. Instead Adi Jr. was glumly leaning by the door and Baba, looking extremely grave, told us He was sad to hear that Margaret, of all people, had told an Eastern disciple that Baba was only holding His birthday celebrations to impress the Westerners and that I had agreed. We should know, He told us, that He did not need to impress anybody.

Of course, this made Margaret and me sob our hearts out. We had made some jokey remark to some Eastern disciples and they had been so shocked they had reported it to Baba, who had used this as a pretext to stir us up. But eventually He took us by the hand, led us into the dining room where the others were waiting wondering what Margaret and Delia had done, and told us to forget it and eat up our ice cream.

Our contribution toward the preparations for the birthday

was tying up the bundles of grain which Baba was to give out to the poor. I received another rebuke over this. When Baba asked Kitty if we had all done our best, Kitty, being scrupulously honest, told Him that I hadn't. Baba spelled out, "Lazy" on the board. I was furious with Kitty and felt this was totally unjustified, but I did not answer or try to justify myself. Eventually it did come to dawn on me that He was right, because, although I could work tirelessly on a task that interested me, on other things I could be less than enthusiastic; and I came to see that Baba might have been trying to egg me on to be more dynamic and energetic.

On the day of Baba's birthday, I will never forget the sight of Him distributing those thousands and thousands of bundles to the destitute, including lepers. As He gave each a bundle from the huge pile on the platform at His side, He touched their feet with His hands. Later He said, "As Baba, I gave; as those wrecks, I received." Sitting in front, watching the *darshan*, was a poignant experience for both His Eastern and Western disciples. It continued all day, from eight in the morning, as the ten thousand filed past Baba. There was only one break when we all sat on the ground and had a meal with Him, but His kindness, thoughtfulness, and humor were always in evidence, hour after hour. As Jean says in *Avatar*:

> We had witnessed the continual outpouring of Baba's benediction upon these human derelicts. Simply to sit in the audience as a spectator of the bountiful love and mercy which one could see and feel emanating from Baba was a soul-stirring experience which moved some of us to tears. Light and darkness, pain and joy mingled in a symphony of human heartbeats as the

compassionate hands of the Master reached down to
the level of humanity's affliction.

The next day was a celebration for Baba's disciples, both
Eastern and Western. His Mohammedan disciples put a cloak of
jasmine and roses on Him and others placed garlands around His
neck. Then, started by His spiritual mother, Gulmai, there was a
ceremony where milk and honey, followed by a little water, were
poured over His feet and about two hundred of us filed past to
have the honor of thus washing His feet. Baba explained:

> The feet, which are physically the lowest part of the
> body, are spiritually the highest. Physically the feet go
> through everything, the good and the bad, the beauti-
> ful and the ugly, the clean and the dirty, yet they are
> above everything. Spiritually the feet of the Master are
> above everything in the Universe, which is like dust to
> Him. When people come to a Perfect Master and touch
> His feet with their heads, they lay upon Him the
> burden of their *sanskaras*—those subtle impressions of
> thought and emotion and action which bind the indi-
> vidual soul to recurrent earthly lives. This is the burden
> to which Jesus referred when He said, "Come unto Me
> all ye who labor and are heavy laden and I will give you
> rest." A Master collects these *sanskaras* from all over
> the Universe, just as an ordinary person in walking
> collects dust on his feet. Those who love Him deeply
> and wish to share His burden as much as possible wash
> His feet with honey, milk, and water which represent
> different types of *sanskaras* and place at His feet a

coconut which symbolizes the complete surrender of their wills to Him.

In the evening, there were speeches by both Eastern and Western disciples, dances and music; and a well-known singer, Master Krishna, came and sang for Baba. This recital lasted for several hours and although we tried to keep awake, it had been a tiring day, and a few of the Westerners fell asleep. So those memorable two days of celebration ended. Baba had looked so beautiful and had given so much, not only to the "wrecks," but also to us.

Sadly, more trouble soon flared up between us in the ashram. There was a showdown between Norina and Jean—Jean objecting to Norina's housekeeping. Baba, as He always did on such occasions, called us all together and told us to thrash it out, keeping nothing hidden. After hearing both sides, usually telling us we must give and take, He would give His ruling. On this occasion, with His usual charm and tact, He appointed Ruano as housekeeper, telling Norina He had a special role for her in the future.

But these upheavals, in which we were all involved, were to break up the Nasik Ashram and bring our stay in India to a close. A meeting was held to decide where we would be together next and Cannes in the south of France was selected. Baba planned to bring the Eastern women on their first trip to the West and the task of finding proper accommodation for them, Baba, the men *mandali*, and the Westerners was entrusted to Kitty.

After a last trip to the house on the hill at Meherabad, to bid a sad farewell to the Eastern women, Margaret, Kitty, and I left Nasik with Baba and went with Him to stay with Kaka's family in Bombay, while we waited for the boat. He took us one evening to the cinema and treated us to our favorite ice cream—coconut for me and mango for Margaret. But all too soon it was time to board the ship for Europe where we were joined by the Backetts and Tom Sharpley.

And so this extraordinary stay in India ended, where the West had been brought to the East and there had been, on all levels, such mixing up. This was to continue with Baba bringing not only the Eastern women to the West on His next trip, but also the *mast* Mohammed, who we had already met on our excursion to the *mast* ashram and who was one of the few *masts* Baba kept with Him permanently. All this at the start of a period of unparalleled upheaval and cruelty in Europe with the coming to power in Germany of the Nazi party.

Back in Britain, we were given instructions while we waited for Baba and the others to arrive from India: Margaret was told that she was to continue running her ballet school; Kitty saw her family to make some financial arrangements; and I was in time to stay with my aunt while my mother was in America on a visit.

With all my love
my darling Leila

M S Grain

P. & O. TURBO-ELECTRIC SHIP "STRATHNAVER," 22,500 TONS

TOURIST CLASS DINING SALOON

TOURIST CLASS LOUNGE

TOURIST CLASS CHILDREN'S NURSERY

TOURIST CLASS TWO-BERTH CABIN

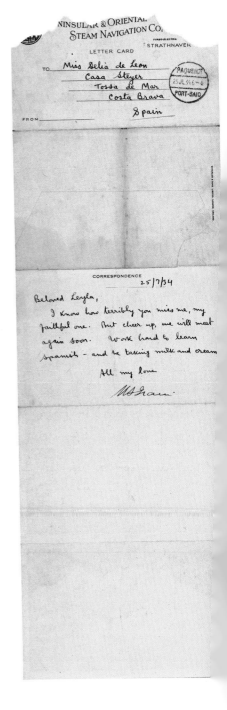

PENINSULAR & ORIENTAL
STEAM NAVIGATION CO.
TURBO-ELECTRIC
STRATHNAVER
LETTER CARD

TO   Miss Delia de Leon
Casa Steyer
Tossa de Mar
Costa Brava

FROM

Spain

CORRESPONDENCE
25/7/34

Beloved Leyla,
I know how terribly you miss me, my faithful one. But cheer up, we will meet again soon. Work hard to learn Spanish — and be taking milk and cream

All my love

M. S. Iran.

Postcards from Meher Baba to Delia

P. & O. TURBO-ELECTRIC SHIP "VICEROY OF INDIA", 20,000 TONS

PORTION OF FIRST CLASS DINING SALOON

FIRST SALOON MUSIC ROOM

A CORNER OF THE FIRST SALOON SMOKING ROOM

THE POMPEIAN SWIMMING BATH

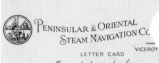

PENINSULAR & ORIENTAL
STEAM NAVIGATION CO

VICEROY

LETTER CARD

TO Miss Delia De Leon
55 Tombayne Gardens
Hampstead
LONDON- N.W.6

FROM _____

CORRESPONDENCE

At Sea — Nov. 12th

My ever-faithful dearest darling Leyla —

We arrive Bombay early Morning 14th.

The voyage, though comfortable, was rather boring, as I missed the love and company of my dearest.

I know how you have been feeling and missing your beloved darling. But this is all going to end now, after six months. Rest assured, and I want you all to give serious attention to the film work I have allotted to each of you, and not to feel sad or dejected. You know how I love you, and want you to be always happy, and love you to be with me, but for the great work that lies ahead, all must put up with some pains. Our happy re-union after six months will be all the more sweeter for the separation you now feel and suffer for me. I know it. So, my dearest Leila, be a good darling, and in the thoughts of a happy re-union after six months, and of the great work you have to do for your beloved B. be happy and keep cheerful. There is no need now to tell you I am always with you, for I AM with you always, as you are with me, for ever and for ever. You know that.

My unbounded love, and loving xxxxxx go with this for my beloved Leila.

Ever Yours

M S Irani

You get a bit fat and strong.

If I don't write for the first fortnight in India due to pressure of work, don't you worry, darling. I will be writing separately, after 15 days.

On her Maiden Voyage — with BABA on board!

THE SS MONTEREY. 632 FEET LONG; 79 FEET BREADTH; GROSS TONNAGE 19,000; SPEED 20½ KNOTS

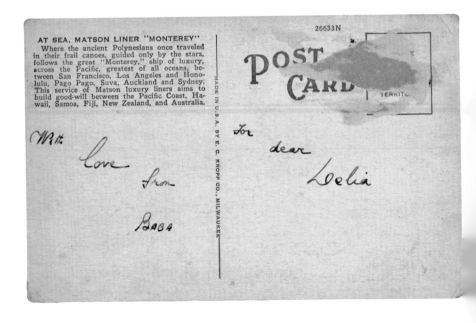

AT SEA, MATSON LINER "MONTEREY"

Where the ancient Polynesians once traveled in their frail canoes, guided only by the stars, follows the great "Monterey," ship of luxury, across the Pacific, greatest of all oceans, between San Francisco, Los Angeles and Honolulu, Pago Pago, Suva, Auckland and Sydney. This service of Matson luxury liners aims to build good-will between the Pacific Coast, Hawaii, Samoa, Fiji, New Zealand, and Australia.

26633N

POST CARD

MADE IN U.S.A. BY E. C. KROPP CO., MILWAUKEE

TERRITO...

With Love from BABA

For dear Leslia

Darling Leila —
I love you

CARTOLINA POSTALE

Once, a charming, sweet girl
fell madly in love with the Lord of the
Universe, and thought she meant very
little to him. But one day she found out
how much He cared for her, and then
became happy for ever.
(Story of Leila & Baba)
....
I didn't receive your letter
sent to Cairo and how I longed to
have it?

M S Irani

To
Darling
Leila
With
All My love
From   BABA

S/S. ESPERIA.

Miss Delia S. de Leon
555 Compayne Gardens
Hampstead
London. N.W.
England asia

Naples . Sunday

All my love to you – beloved
Leyla – pure and faithful in
love, for the Divine Beloved
that is me. Think of the happy
reunion, darling secretary!

U.S. Gram

Nuestro Señor Crucificado.
Velázquez.   Museo del Prado, 1167.

Fot. Hauser y Menet.- Madrid.

With all my love

~Abram~

Miss *Debra de Leon*

55 Compayne Gardens

N.W. 6

LONDON

England

Cairo — Memorials of 4000 Years Ago, the Pyramids of Gizeh. 431

Oh you Mad lover of Mine
No longer Must you think
I neglect my faithful
dear one who is amongst
those who are closest
to me

U S Grant

Union Postale

POST CARD

Egypt

PUBL. THE ORIENTAL COMMERCIAL BUREAU
PORT SAID (EGYPT)

To

Leila
with all My love

from

Baba

CAIRO
Les trois Grandes Pyramides de Gizeh
Die drei großen Pyramiden von Gizeh

Cairo   Moslems Morning Prayer near Pyramids   426

Leyla

Union Postale
POST CARD
Egypt

Darling Leyla – we leave here on
Jan 3rd/33 for Colombo, on the Balæran
arriving there Jan 12" — will you write
there for one week c/o Cooks, Colombo,
& then to the address in Lasik.
All my love
M S Mani

PUBL. THE ORIENTAL COMMERCIAL BUREAU
PORT SAID (EGYPT)

CAIRO
La Prière du Matin près des Pyramides
Morgengebet bei den Pyramiden

BARCELONA - 127   PLAÇA D'ESPANYA   PLAZA DE ESPAÑA   PLACE D'ESPAGNE

All my love.

Mabran.

Miss Delia De Leon

55. Campagne Gardens

Hampstead.

London.

England.

Boats laden with Coral from the Maldive Islands at anchor near Mount Lavinia, Ceylon.

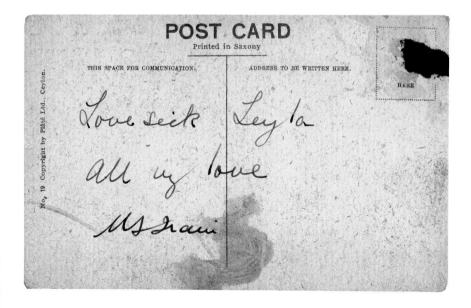

POST CARD

Printed in Saxony

THIS SPACE FOR COMMUNICATION.

ADDRESS TO BE WRITTEN HERE.

HERE

Love sick Leyla

All my love

Ms Irani

OZEAN-BRIEF
OCEAN-LETTER ★ CARTA DE ALTA MAR

Aufgenommen auf		Lfd. Nr.
D. Europa dans		
am 1801 15MAI82		115
um	be	
durch		

| Von D From S.S. Del vapore | BREMEN DDAS | Nr. 25 | 15/25 |

delia de leon
55 compayne gardens
hampstead
london nw 6

read letter expressing silent deep yearnings of your
heart for nearness of divine beloved love

Debeg Nr. 17. 10000. 7. 31. HPL. ★

Bitte wenden
P. T. O.
a la vuelta

POST ✦ OFFICE
TELEGRAM

No.

OFFICE STAMP

3 JLY 40

Prefix. Time handed in. Office of Origin and Service Instructions. Words

From

m
20

To

120   C 1.425   AHMEDNAGAR   33

NLT- DELIA DELEON PINEACRES CHURCH ROAD HINDHEAD =

ARE YOU MARY WILL SHARPLEY READY TO OBEY ME IMPLICITLY

DURING MY LAST YEAR OF SILENCE COMMENCING FIRST AUGUST

ENDING 31 JULY 1941 CABLE REPLY = MEHERBABA ＋ ＋

31 1941 ＋ ＋

For free repetition of doubtful words telephone "TELEGRAMS ENQUIRY" or call, with this form
at office of delivery. Other enquiries should be accompanied by this form and, if possible, the envelope.

Cables from Meher Baba to Delia

IMPERIAL AND INTERNATIONAL COMMUNICATIONS LIMITED

IMPERIAL AND EMPIRADIO TELEGRAPH SERVICES

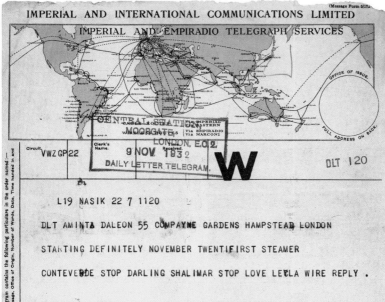

CENTRAL STATION
MOORGATE
LONDON, E.C.2.
IMPERIAL
Via EMPIRADIO
Via MARCONI

9 NOV 1932

Received.

DAILY LETTER TELEGRAM.

W

Circuit. VWZ GP 22   Clerk's Name.   DLT 120

L19 NASIK 22 7 1120

DLT AMINTA DALEON 55 COMPAYNE GARDENS HAMPSTEAD LONDON

STARTING DEFINITELY NOVEMBER TWENTIFIRST STEAMER

CONTEVERDE STOP DARLING SHALIMAR STOP LOVE LEELA WIRE REPLY .

K19 55

CABLE AND WIRELESS
LIMITED

"Via Imperial"

CABLE ROUTES
WIRELESS ROUTES

OFFICE OF ISSUE
1 MAR
CENTRAL
FULL ADDRESS ON BACK

2346

Circuit.   Clerk's Name.   Time Received.   1581

K120 G MAHABALESHWAR 18 28 1730 =

LC DELIA DELEON FLORENCE NIGHTINGALE HOSTEL

SISSONGROVE LNNW1 =

LOVE TO YOU MINTA ENAWILL MARY AND ALL OTHERS =

MEHERBABA

Shanghai June 27, 1932

My darling Delia,

You must have read the diary of events written by Chanji for Kimco. We arrived Shanghai on the 22nd and were received on the boat by Kitty's brother Herbert. After a day and a half in Shanghai we went [...] for a few [...] week in c[...] Herbert w[...] I am sen[...] Liberia. [...] July. [...] Genoa w[...] July. Yo[...] will com[...] 29th[...] I know [...]

CABLE ADDRESS—MUSCHENHEIM—NEW YORK

Hotel Astor
TIMES SQUARE
New York

FRED. A. MUSCHENHEIM

28/11/31

Dearest Delia
just received your letter and poems, dont worry we received all your letters and poems.
We are leaving New york fo[r] Harmon to night, and w[e] are sailing from New Yo[rk]

Letters from Meher Baba to Delia

MEHERABAD

Ahmednagar — Dec. 11, 1937

My ever dearest and faithful Leyla,

Moana Hotel
Royal Hawaiian Hotel
Seaside Hotel

ADDRESS ALL
COMMUNICATIONS
TO THE MANAGER

MOANA HOTEL
HONOLULU
CABLE ADDRESS "MOANA"

June 10th 1932

Dear Delia —

Baba received your letters. There is
No need to explain to you how pleased He was to read
those ...

$$ "AUSONIA"

PIROSCAFO "AUSONIA"

At Sea
22nd Aug. 1932

LLOYD TRIESTINO

Dearest Leila — Your Note was handed to me by Keka.
It touched Me so deeply to read it. I knew it all for a
fact how deep were your feelings and how intense your
love for Me. You seem to think and feel Neglected
and Sad, but as I already explained to you, it is not
so. I love You, my Leila, as deeply and as intensely
as I love Khalimar or others, and if, for reasons, it is not
outwardly expressed, it must not & does not mean
otherwise — I know and am so glad to see that you
have always been "My Faithful" one — always wanting
to see Me happy. And whenever I felt like sad or in
mood, you felt it so keenly, & miserable and cried or
tried all your best to make Me happy again ...... How can
I forget it all? I know all, and know all the while
how intensely & immensely you love Me, and if you do
not know Now how deep and great my love is for my
Leila. You will one day know it for certain.
Meanwhile, don't at all worry. The feeling of
Separation is so keen this time. I too feel it so much but the

Meherabad
Ahmednagar, April 14.

My ever faithful darling Leyla,

I have all your letters, the last
enquiringabout going to Spain and about
learning shorthand. Yes, dearest, you can go
to Spain, and also study shorthand. In short
I want you to be busym and in any way keep
yourself cheerful and happy under all conditions.

Yes, the great moment is now approach
-ing, and this last intervening period is one
of suffering, for me and also for those who
are mine. And whenever you have to face
things and facts that pain and puzzle you,
remember you are mine. That will enable you
to stand anything boldly, and cheerfully. I
know you will, with allyour heart, for you
are my ever faithful and beloved Leyla.

I am busy arranging things prior to
my retirement, but any way remember I want you
to be writing to me wherever I am even on
the Himalayas, for I shall be intouch with you
my dearest gopies even through correspondence
although as a matter of fact, I am always with
you in spirit. Distancesinspace and delays
in correesppondence do not matter where love
binds the dearest ones in a bond that is ever
inseparable! And you, my ever dearest Leyla,
are so close at heart and so constant in my
thoughts too.

The film work, asreported from the
other end, is progressing gradually.

All my love

remember dearest I am always with You
and You belong to me, for ever

M.S. Irani

A MOMENTOUS VISIT

 In August 1937, I joined Kitty in Marseilles to be there to meet Baba and the party when they arrived from India—Adi Sr. followed later with Mohammed. It was the first visit to the West for the Eastern women. Mani's diary describes their trip in detail and with her permission I have quoted parts of it here to give some of the flavor. Mehera, at this time, was in strict seclusion from men and so the only time she had been able to take the air on the boat was in the early hours of the morning, the rest of the time being spent in the cabin below decks.

JULY 29 – Six of us with Baba left Meherabad 2:50 by car for Vilad Station. Reached Bombay early hours of morning. Stopped at Regent Hotel—Rano, Norina, Nonny, and Elizabeth also there.

JULY 31 – Left hotel 7:30 a.m. and after medical examination went to Strathnaver 8:30 a.m. Started sailing 1:20 p.m.—rough weather.

AUGUST 1 – On deck for an hour from 5:30 a.m. Mehera seasick and miserable.

AUGUST 2 – Rougher weather. All seasick.

AUGUST 4 – Better. Stopped at Aden 3:15 p.m. and were out on deck to see the fascinating colors of the lights playing on the rippling waters and noisy little piscie boats riding gaily on the waves.... At night we entered the Red Sea.

AUGUST 5 – Went up First Class deck from 4:25 to 5:30 a.m., groping in the dark to climb the endless stairs but very lovely up there with the bracing wind—Red Sea was hot! Rough weather—portholes closed—played cards and other games in cabin. Some of us sick.

AUGUST 6 – Went up on deck 4:10 a.m. and reached Port Sudan 12 p.m.

AUGUST 7 – Went up on deck 2:30 a.m. and slept there till 4:45. Every day Mehera not well in spite of pills and things Baba gave.

AUGUST 8 – Crossed the Suez Canal at 7:30 a.m. and so contrary to the hitherto unsteady sailing went gliding like a bird on the strip of sky-blue water. We watched from both decks—Arabia with its deserts and camels on one side, and Egypt on the other.

AUGUST 9 – Mehera ill all night.

AUGUST 10 – Weather much better.

AUGUST 11 – At 12 sighted Italy, at 2 Masina, and at

4 p.m. Stromboli Volcano (smoking).

AUGUST 12 – Mehera feeling nice today. Sighted Corsica at 1:40 (Sardinia on other side). Did packing.

AUGUST 13 – Reached Marseilles at 6 a.m. (Kitty and Delia received us) and left boat 7:40 a.m. for hotel. Went off to see zoo at 9:10. Had splendid lunch at hotel and left by train for Cannes (2nd class). After a very pleasant journey of about three and a half hours we reached Cannes. Shelly House, where we stopped for two nights and one day—an ancient fairy-tale house full of mysterious echoes and antique furniture and a spacious garden.

AUGUST 15 – Left Shelly for Villa Caldana (Madame and her cat welcomed us—nice big house—lovely garden terrace).

AUGUST 16 – Before supper walked through the woods belonging to the house.

So we all were in Cannes together. Baba, the Eastern women, Kitty, Elizabeth, Rano, and Norina stayed in the villa on the hill and the rest of us were housed in a large villa with two small bungalows. Apart from Anita, Mabel, Nonny, Tom Sharpley, the Backetts, and Sam Cohen, there were many other visitors who came for short periods—the Mertens, Anna Caterina, Consuelo and Alfredo Sides, Gita (Norina's sister), Mercedes da Costa, Vicky and Alice Traum from Vienna, an opera singer from the Opera House, who was full of sparkle and always tripping about on very high heels, singing, which amused Baba.

He told us we must continue the search for the perfect boy, telling us again that when he was found He would break His silence. Kitty produced a rather ugly Spanish refugee boy whom Baba kept for a few days and then sent away. Dr. Donkin also brought a boy but this one was not right either.

One evening Baba, wearing a beret and a cape belonging to Mercedes, went into Monte Carlo and watched the gambling at the famous Casino there—this must have affected gambling activity throughout the world.

At this time, Mabel was very ill and spent most of the time in bed. Mary looked after her devotedly and Baba came every day to see her. None of us realized how ill she really was, but eventually Margaret was asked to take her home and Donkin went to help them on the journey.

During this time Anita and I became close friends. We were put together by Baba and we would often make Him laugh—this indeed was Anita's special quality. One day Baba sent us to search for a beach that was secluded and where the women could go without being seen by any men. On our return, when we excitedly entered into the room, Baba had been giving interviews and was looking very solemn. Anita, rushing to Him, tripped and fell sprawling at His feet, which caused Baba to laugh heartily, saying it was just what He had needed.

Later Anita told Baba about Roger Vieillard, an artist specializing in etching and engraving she had met at art classes and who wanted to marry her. Baba was in favor of the match and eventually Roger became a devoted disciple.

Again from Mani's diary:

AUGUST 21 – Baba went with Norina to Monte

Carlo; Delia, Anita, Christine came to lunch.

AUGUST 23 – In morning went to the beach (secluded spot); Westerners had a swim.

AUGUST 24 – Anna Caterina and Anita joined at "work." In the evening went to Palm Beach and saw heavenly fireworks. Left Him at 9 p.m., but had to wait there four hours before fireworks started (had a topping time with Baba) at 1:20 a.m. for 20 minutes. Reached home 2:20 a.m.

AUGUST 26 – Delia, Margaret, and Anita visit.

AUGUST 28 – Kitty's birthday. Had a grand dinner party up on terrace (Naja's foot in the steaming cauliflower accident).

AUGUST 29 – Kitty leaves for Paris—walks.

AUGUST 30 – Drizzly weather.

AUGUST 31 – Kitty returned from Paris—we played "darts."

SEPTEMBER 1 – Indian music and darts. Ruano and Nonny came for the evening.

SEPTEMBER 3 – Played with Baba—darts after lunch, and Spanish records and charades after supper.

SEPTEMBER 4 – Anita and Delia visit—in the evening played with Baba charades and grey ghost, followed by coffee and cakes (Irene Billo made them).

SEPTEMBER 5 – Played with Baba, darts, bagetelles,

and treasure hunt (heaps of fun).

SEPTEMBER 7 – Nonny, Delia, and Anita visit—played charades.

SEPTEMBER 8 – In the afternoon we all fixed the big bed in Baba's room (the room where Baba works every morning for two hours)—bicycle rides in garden.

SEPTEMBER 9 – Anita and Delia visit. Charades and music after supper.

SEPTEMBER 10 – Liza arrived. Played treasure hunt with Baba. I had a "tap" lesson.

SEPTEMBER 11 – Rano sketched Mehera's portrait. After supper played charades and music by the fireside as cold and rainy.

SEPTEMBER 12 – Mehera took piano lessons from Kitty.

SEPTEMBER 13 – Cycling and walks.

SEPTEMBER 14 – In the evening played "Abjunkin and Clumps" with Baba—rainy.

SEPTEMBER 15 – Nice and sunny—cycling and walks. In the evening played charades and "murder" game by the fireside in the drawing room.

SEPTEMBER 16 – Rainy—windy.

SEPTEMBER 17 – Ruano's birthday. Had birthday supper by candlelight and played music and "musical chairs" and had a little entertainment by Anita, Rano, and self.

SEPTEMBER 18 – Baba spent day at Capo de Monte.

Anita and I paid many visits to the house on the hill, where we often played charades. Baba would sometimes take part Himself and, of course, we all wanted to be on His side. I remember Him once playing a surgeon operating on different ones in turn, which must have had some effect on the deeper levels of our vices and virtues. And then there was Mani who was a theater in herself: she wrote her own sketches, peopling the stage with different characters, sometimes singing or dancing. Those were such lovely occasions.

One day Baba told us that Mehera would like to have a bicycle and as she had never asked for anything before He would like her to have her wish so we clubbed together to hire one and we all enjoyed seeing her riding through the grounds of the villa.

It was strange how, when you least expected it, Baba would be touched by some little gesture and be extra tender. Once I gave Him a novelty powder compact with a watch in it and said, "For Mehera, or anyone else you like." He gave me a loving look and kiss and there were almost tears in those wonderful eyes. It seemed nothing to me, but somehow it touched Him. On the other hand, at times when I thought I might be praised, I was often ignored.

So our visit to Cannes now too came to an end. We all realized that this had been a momentous visit with the coming to the West of the Eastern women. The World's Fair had been on in Paris and Baba took the Eastern women and Norina to stay for three days at Consuelo Sides's flat there. We can only imagine how He must have been working on the changes that were soon to happen to all those nations represented there. On top of this Baba had brought Mohammed, whom He said represented Germany. All this seemed to presage the world upheaval and enormous psychological changes that were soon to come.

When, in October, Baba returned to India He took with Him Kitty, Rano, Norina, and Elizabeth. The rest of us went our separate ways but He told us that, should war break out, Margaret and I were to come to Him in India. It was sad to say goodbye, but I would have been much sadder at the parting if I had known that I would not actually be seeing Him again until 1948.

"...JUST LOVE ME"

This long separation and later the war were miserable experiences through which Baba's letters would shine—as always dictated by Baba and written down by Chanji.

Meherabad
Ahmednagar
December 15, 1937

Dearest Leyla,

(When it is Baba writing to you, then you are always Leyla. When I write on my own, then Delia simply. Baba wrote about ten days ago, only the letter went by ordinary mail. He received your letter two days ago. He is glad you found Mabel so cheerful and bright.)

Yes, Margaret is having a hellish time with her people, but one thing is certain, Mabel will never leave Me. She will grow closer to Me right up to the end. Talking of the West the other evening, I said there were three things in the West I liked—Kimco, Assisi, and

Portofino—so you need never fear that Kimco will slip from the very precious place in My heart. As I have said before, each is as I made and want each to be and, even when they are troublesome, sometimes the fault is not entirely theirs, although I want each of you to try your best to control when I ask.

If you love Me as I know you do and you understand My workings, then it is easy and possible.

I am glad you remembered the words I said some years ago to you. They apply as much to the present as they did at the time I gave you them.

Don't be discouraged—don't worry, but be gay and happy and be your old self when I come to the West again.

All My love to you, My darling Leyla, and love to your mother.

M. S. IRANI

We were all worried about Mabel; she had cancer and her health was fast deteriorating, so we wrote to Baba and He wrote back:

Meherabad
January 2, 1938

...I was very touched to read how much you all want Me to come to London soon and see Mabel. You know how dear to My heart Kimco are, and always will be, and I would never refuse them anything that was at all possible, and that did not interfere with My work.

However, all rest assured that I am very near Mabel, and I want you and others to feel Me near and in you as Mabel does. She draws daily closer to Me—and is becoming daily more completely filled with Me alone....

Sadly, Mabel died soon afterward. She was much loved for her warmth of character, gaiety, and humor and so we all missed her very much. Not long after it was Baba's Birthday and Kimco sent Him a present:

> Meherabad
> Ahmednagar
> February 22, 1938

My darling Leyla,

And what surprises from My beloved Kimco! A special birthday letter of love for your Beloved Baba—a special cable of love—and a loving thought behind the "surprise packet" from Bombay. The very things I wanted. Bay rum, Cuticura soap, and soft handkerchiefs.

You will all hear later from Kitty about the birthday itself. After today all the festivities will be finished and we shall be busy preparing for our three months at Panchgani. We go there on the 12th March. Still be sending all cables and letters here as usual. All will be forwarded.

I know how you feel parting with dear Mabel. But Mabel has not parted from you. She is closer to you now than she ever was or could be before. *Love knows no separation* and because you loved her so much, nothing—not even death, as physical separation is called—can break that tie of love there is between you.

Be happy in the thought that Mabel is happy. She sees Me all the time. She is near Me and in a very short while will be physically near Me, too. This has to be, as she is of My Circle.

I note what you say about your health. Take whatever the doctor advises. Get well as quickly as you can. Your feeling you need Me is really My *need of you*. None realize how much I need those whom I have chosen for future work. You may feel you are struggling through *maya* alone, but is this really so? Are you ever separated from Me? I am nearer you in the spot to which I have sent you than I would be if you were here and I had not asked you to be here.

But struggle is good. Without it where would *maya* and illusion be defeated?

M. S. IRANI

I was still a bit jealous of the extra attention I thought Baba gave to Minta and Margaret, and I suppose my letters reflected that.

Panchgani
May 11, 1938

Dearest Leyla,
So you feel disappointed I did not write to you when I wrote to Margaret and Minta! And today comes

another letter from you full of love for your Beloved Baba! Your last letter but one must have been written on one of your "bad mood" days, as you say!

But one thing makes Me happy. In spite of My long silence you always remember to write to Me every week. Are you not My faithful Leyla?

I am just back from Meherabad having given instructions for a larger room to be built on the top of the present building to accommodate ten to twelve more people. Also a garage for Elizabeth's car. If there are sufficient funds there will be a hospital just outside the compound where sick people and babies will be cared for. This will be run in conjunction with the work already started down below.

I went to Bangalore a week ago, and had we had sufficient funds I should have moved all My work there and have called My beloved Kimco to join Me there. But now this won't be till eight months. So, in the meantime keep happy and do your best to get well, strong, and plump.

Here it is lovely weather—only 84 to 88 degrees. Yesterday in Meherabad it was 105. We shall probably be here all July as the necessary decorations in Meherabad will not be completed to allow Me to return there earlier.

I know how much you long for your "dear Baba" to come to the West. But this cannot be for the present, as I have much work to do here, and the time for My speaking is drawing very near. Then the whole world will be My sphere of work.

Be loving Me—all of you—with all the love you are capable of. As the great event draws nearer, I need the love of all My Circle. You cannot know how much your love means to Me and how much I long to have you near Me, but you will be with Me soon.

I send love to your dear mother.

All My love,
M. S. IRANI

As usual, Baba was able to cheer me up through His letters.

Panchgani
May 29, 1938

Dearest Leyla,

Your letter, received yesterday, in answer to My last, made Me so happy. It struck a much happier note than the previous one.

You have grown so much in your understanding and realize that all I do and all I make each of you suffer is only to draw you closer in love to Me—your Beloved. Could I bear to see you all suffer if it were not that the goal to which it is leading you is "the pearl of great price," "the love that passeth all understanding."

Why are you one of the Circle? Because you have within you the very thing you now so earnestly desire—the capacity to love—and to love to the very end. And when this power to love has reached its perfected state, i.e., without any thought of self, then you will experience a happiness beyond anything you have as yet experienced. This is Union. Love for the Beloved, free from self.

It is in the effort you are making to control your moods and emotions and to get above these dark periods that has made you feel Me so near. You are right when you say, "I haunt you," so that your longing and desire for Me have become increasingly intensified. Why? Is it not I who all the time am this desire and longing? You are Mine and it is Myself in you I love. Is not the struggle worthwhile? To see ever more and more of Myself in My faithful Leyla to love?

And I promise you what you ask. As you struggle for this control so too you will grow calmer and more balanced.

I am happy that you are doing all you can to make your mother happy. She is all you say she is and much more besides.

I know you are ready to come to me whenever I send for you. In the meantime, you are doing all I told you to do. Get strong and keep well and fit. Eat well, sleep well, and above all let nothing worry you. Am I not always with you?

All My love,
M. S. IRANI

At this time, rumors of what was happening in Germany and fears that this would eventually lead to war were rife. Commenting on the world situation in His next letter, Baba said:

... The world is in a state of fear and perplexity. No

one knows what is going to happen. But wait and see. I know all—the present and the future—and nothing can stop the work that I am here to do. Am I not the Avatar and the world will know it soon and will accept Me as such. Be patient. Be calm. Be steady and firm as a rock in your faith and love for Me. I can then use you as a channel for My work—the work of Divine Love for the upliftment of all humanity.

As you know, I need none of you. I can work My Will independently, but I have chosen for My own reasons a few to help Me in that work. But these few need a love and faith as rare as that of St. Francis. Let this same love of his for Christ be your goal and love Me as he loved his Master.

> All My love,
> (Sgn) M. S. IRANI
> (this was Baba's signature)

Baba would refer to St. Francis' love for Christ again and again, but this letter also upset me and I wrote to Baba asking about *sanskaras*; why we had so many weaknesses and why certain people were destined to leave Him? With His usual patience He wrote back, reassuring me:

> Meherabad
> Ahmednagar
> November 5, 1938

Dearest Leyla,
So you received a cold letter of welcome from your

darling Baba. That was too bad. But have you not misunderstood My words?

It is true that I need no disciples here or elsewhere. I can do My work alone through the heart of man without choosing a few selected ones. But in this Avataric period as in the time of Jesus, I chose to live in close contact with Me (either here or elsewhere does not matter) those who have been with Me from ages past and who love Me deeply and whom I have loved since eternity.

Still this does not prevent My saying, "I can carry on My work without you." All of you could leave Me, but the world would go on. It would be harder for Me—it would be a crucifixion but nevertheless the work of love would not suffer. Nothing can stop God's work. If My own refuse or disappoint Me, I must get the work done through some other medium.

But I would suffer, so My faithful Leyla must never let Me down, but stick it right to the bitter end, whatever hardship may be in store. Why did I call you the "Faithful Leyla?" Not for no reason.

You know, in spite of what you say in your letter that nothing can separate you or all mankind from Me, because I am in all and God cannot be separated from Himself, can He? But as I have so often explained, that just as the eye or the ear may be more useful and necessary to a man than, say, his sense of smell or touch, so some are more necessary to Me for My present work than others. I say now as always, "Kimco is My heart and will remain forever My heart" wherever they are and you know the value of the heart to the body. Without it man in the human form could not exist and I too without My heart would feel part of Me was missing. Have I not shown you many times, both in the past and now, how deeply I love you and I know how much you are capable of feeling My love at certain moments, when I wish it so. I know the inner growth of each. Must I further demonstrate My love to convince you? Where would your faith come in?

Your third point, are you as I made you? The *sans-karas* you have I gave you to work through for My work, so it is true to say you are as I made you, but the goal still remains for you and all to attain perfection through duality. Remember *maya* is My shadow, so indirectly is Me, too, and is the means by which the soul, divine though it is, but unconscious as yet of its divinity, must become conscious of its oneness with God.

Herein lies the riddle of the Universe and My game, too. Perfect you are because soul is always perfect, being God, but it must wade through duality to attain conscious perfection. And as My Circle is already God-Realized (but the curtain being drawn, are unaware of it), I give them, at the appointed time of birth, these *sanskaras* to work through. Now is it clear? And how can you help in this game of Mine? By love and service. By control of your mind and moods and, yes, weaknesses which are there for the purpose of exercising control over them. Often the greater one's love, the greater is the tendency to moods, because the pangs of separation are more acute. But I do not like moods and therefore to please Me, which is one of the best ways of showing your love for Me, try your best to overcome them.

Now cheer up, My faithful Leyla. I love you as always and you love Me infinitely more than you used to. I will come to the West soon, that I promise you and let Me see you looking plump, well, and happy. A joyful heart will help you most to get strong.

All My love,
M. S. IRANI

Baba always liked us to be cheerful and continually stressed that cheerfulness was a Divine Art, but how patient He was with one's questions and how lovingly He explained at such length.

We held a reunion party at Margaret's flat to which Audrey, who Baba referred to as Shirin, came, although by this time she was no longer involved with the group.

Meherabad
Ahmednagar
November 7, 1938

Dearest Leyla,

I only wrote and posted you a letter two days ago in answer to your previous letter and now today another letter from which you certainly gave Me a big surprise.

I was so happy to receive a joint letter from so many written on the occasion of the reunion party at Margaret's flat and to see among those who were there Shirin's signature. She is still Mine and will one day, when she has exhausted all *maya* has to teach her, come back to Me of her own free will. Like many others, she has work for Me to do in the world. Nothing can snap the "Golden Thread" that love has woven between thee and Me. It may stretch almost to breaking point, but it will not snap. So force nothing. I know My own and where each of them is and when I need them near Me I will call them and they will come.

Christine wrote Me a very happy and honest letter. It made Me very happy. I don't mind what people take Me as, but I do like honesty and truth. I like her to think things out for herself. She came to Me before she quite knew what it was all about. I had My reasons for this. But the only obedience I want from each is that which is the outcome of love and faith.

Be kind and take an interest in her. Am I not interested in all things, however trivial they may seem? Her work I know is dull and monotonous at times.

And now love to My faithful Leyla, who once again has shown her love in the effort she has made to help and please Me.

M. S. IRANI

I was glad that I obeyed Baba and took an interest in Christine as, tragically, she was killed in the early days of the war when a bomb hit the restaurant where she was working. Although I had moved out of London, I would go and see her whenever I came to town; and Margaret, Charles Purdom, and I would often lunch at the London store where she worked and she was always so pleased to see any of us. Although she was not able to accept Baba, what a spiritual blessing she must have had to be so in contact with the Avatar.

So dawned the year 1939, and from Baba came more news and thanks for the Christmas presents we had sent:

Jubblepore
January 11, 1939

Dearest Leyla,

The Christmas cable of love from dearest Kimco pleased Me very much. Tell Shalimar so, but that I was disappointed not to receive a letter from her. All witnessed the unpacking of the Christmas hamper which arrived in perfect condition. We had great fun guessing what the packets contained. "Bay rum," said one when the sweets were unpacked. How pleased to find sweets which all could enjoy! The Snow White records have already been played many times and enjoyed.

The packets of cards you sent for everyone I distributed with My own hands and the girls thank you very much and send their love and good wishes. They often speak of the days in Cannes and the happy evenings spent playing charades.

Tell your mother I am so happy she is planning to take a house outside London. It will be good for her and for your health, too. I send her all My love and blessings. I know how much she loves Me and how difficult life is for her at times. But I will help her always. She must not worry over money or the fear of war. I will look after all who are Mine wherever they are. Just keep on loving and think of Me. Long for what is real. You will then have no time for worrying over what may never happen. Truth and love, which are one, you will find and they will give you permanent happiness. Both are expressions of the One God who is in all and behind all, your Beloved Baba.

You will receive shortly an account of our travels up to the present. The actual tour starts on the 15th of this month, when we leave here and go direct to Benares. Later we go to Kashmir, stopping at Ajmer, Delhi, and Lahore on the way. Karachi we visit on our return. Life is not easy for the group. They see very little of Me. But this is not a holiday trip. I have great work to do and they have all much to learn. Life is a school wherever you are. This, too, you are finding. I teach all whom I have chosen and you, dearest Leyla, are doing your utmost to respond to My works of love. You are right when you say you have much to learn and experience. I will see that you have the experience you need. Half the battle is won when you can face up to yourself as you are doing and can see the false from the true. Truth is within, but is hidden by this false ego. I, the Divine Sculptor of all hearts, will mold the "Perfect One," Myself, whom I love in all.

All My love, dearest Leyla. Two years will soon be up! Keep bright and happy for the sake of your Beloved. I feel every sad thought of My "Kimco" who are forever My heart.

M. S. IRANI

My mother had given up her London flat and taken a large

bungalow in Hinehead in Surrey and, with Baba's consent, I moved down to be with her. In one letter I had sent Baba a translation of a poem by Jacoponi Da Todi, a follower of St. Francis, that Kim and I had included in our little anthology. Baba obviously liked it because He quoted part of it in His next letter:

Bhopal
March 5, 1939

Dearest Faithful Leyla,

Will you forgive your Beloved if He writes you a birthday letter one month late? He will make up for it by sending you an extra loving thought with each line. You will remember He told you how busy He would be on this tour and, apart from correspondence connected with the tour and the work He has to do on this tour, He has written no letters whatsoever. Now is He forgiven? Write by return and tell Him so or He will mourn, grow thin and haggard, and will never be able to take the long tiring journey to the West which He longs to take shortly to see again His beloved Kimco—His heart.

And now there lie before Me so many of My dearest Leyla's letters. I do not know which to answer first. But amongst the letters I see there is that beautiful poem translated from the Italian which I loved so much that I had it read aloud twice and translated so that all might understand its meaning. Hear part of it again:

If he offer thee his embrace run his caress
   to meet
If not his withholding is sweet

If thou has served him well given him all
  that was thine
Loved only the Divine he never will part
  from thee
Wholly in him shalt thou dwell.

I was staying at Ajmer—a spot I love so much because of its natural beauty and its spiritual atmosphere—and for one night I took all up to the mountains to the tomb of Piran Pir, a great Mohammedan saint. It was a most beautiful spot—the finest view we have so far seen on the tour. I had work to do there and it was here in this beautiful spot that I called all together and had your poem read aloud.

Now another letter and your birthday letter, full of loving kisses. Yes and the nice handkerchiefs from you and Margaret jointly. The same day I began using them. And the cable I also received on the same day—no celebration at all—just work with the beggars on the spiritual path.

I did receive a letter from Quentin Tod. You ask if I received one. I am happy you liked My article in the second number of the magazine. When are you going to send Me an article? Kimco are lazy. They do not write for the magazine and I know they could if they tried.

I am glad your mother has found a nice house out of London. Be out in the air and walk every day. Look your best when I come. I know what a lot you have been through these last two years, but not in vain. You have profited and learned much. It will be a changed Leyla, but yet the same Leyla. You have helped Me a lot by cooperation and not "kicking against the pricks." I would love to have had you here with Me, but you say truly, "there are lessons that must be learned even apart from the physical presence of the Master." I teach you wherever you are. But not all make it so easy for Me to teach them as you have done by trying to understand My ways and yourself better. You love Me as few do and, because of this deep love, I can test you by putting so much on you to work through and overcome for My sake.

In My conscious state I limit Myself, so too in the conscious state of My Circle, I set also limits and when I choose I free them from those limits—but in My own time. Until then be happy, content, and know it is all My doing. If you could understand but a little how great is My love for you, you would feel all was worthwhile if it is to please your Beloved.

When I draw the curtain you will understand all and smile at My game. It is all illusion. The pain of yesterday is no more—the joy of a week ago is no more—only the present exists and the love you feel for your Beloved. The pain caused from the separation from your Beloved is as real as is the happiness that union with your Beloved is real. But as I have once said, "The unconscious self which is God, to become conscious, has to go through this apparent opposite process of duality to become aware of its oneness with God and give that conscious union with God which makes lover and the Beloved one."

You make the effort and I will give you the victory. It is a divine struggle with purpose behind it. Don't fight against it.

> 'tis in vain the bars to beat
> Effort and struggle are vain

Now write and keep on writing whenever the urge is there. It is love that urges you to write.

All My love to yourself, your mother, and your family.

M. S. IRANI

What keeps amazing me is that Baba, amidst all His travels and work, took the trouble to answer my questions in detail with such patience, kindness, and love. I am also amazed that I, who never asked questions when with Baba, became so loquacious in writing letters to Him and, having been gently ticked off for being lazy, I did sit down and write some articles for the *Meher Baba Journal* and I found it surprisingly easy—one was called *Don't Worry*:

> To be told by Meher Baba not to worry may seem a commonplace and simple thing. Those unaccustomed to His ways or newly meeting Him might wonder why He bothers to mention the obvious, for we all have our worries. Especially it might come as a shock to those who desire to hear from Him learned metaphysical or philosophical discussions. Meher Baba's concern is to awaken the love within us so that we may become really human beings. His appeal is to the heart. Directly and

simply He gets down to the very roots of our being. Invariably He says:

Don't worry; I will help you. Just love Me.

These words, like the words of Jesus*, are deep and significant; for they are a clarion call to us, to rouse ourselves, to awaken from our smug little outlook on life, to yearn for a richer, fuller, deeper way of living.

If we want to understand Meher Baba's ways, we have only to pause and think a little to realize that the fundamental cause of most of the trouble that is shaking the foundations of our world today is worry, and its inevitable sister, fear. Everywhere we see entire nations and peoples in the grip of this worrying business. The life of the individual makes up the life and character of the nation, and each in turn reacts on other peoples and nations. We worry because we lack health, possessions, money, or lands. We poison our lives at the source and that affects our adjustments to each other. Then comes intolerance, greed, and persecution. We have not got the right kind of faith—the faith that helps us recognize the rights and needs of all men to live peacefully in brotherhood and to know that we are all part of the whole.

If we had this faith, we would know, as Hafiz says:

*My peace I give unto you not as the world giveth, give I unto you. Let not your heart be troubled, neither let it be afraid."
                                    —St. John, Chapter 14, Verse 27

The object of all religion is alike—all men
seek their Beloved. O, all the world is love's
dwelling; why talk of a mosque or a church?

Why do we worry so much? With many people it is
because they feel an eternal dissatisfaction. They want
things different; something eludes them always. Small
wonder that in their desperate desire to be free from
worry they follow false gods, thinking they will be led to
Utopia. They are deceived, by words and grandiose
promises, and are "let down" invariably for they fail to
realize that the remedy lies within themselves. It is only
a Perfect One like Meher Baba that can give them the
right answer to all that troubles them and the world
today. He has Himself attained freedom and can help
others to this freedom. If we turn to Him, He will help
us and in Him we can find hope and strength. The very
fact of His telling us, "Don't worry, be happy" helps us
and gives us power, for it loosens up within us the
causes of our worries.

To love Him and to obey Him is the next step—it is
so much easier with Him behind us. For it is a spiritual
solution, and no amount of physical or mental striving
can solve our problems. Meher Baba does help us to
change our attitude to life; and it is not a negative
attitude that Baba asks us to cultivate, but a positive,
joyful acceptance of experiences in their right focus.
Not to be caught up in the passing phases of illusion
(*maya*)—"to be in the world but not of it"—does not
mean a shrinking from life. We have our parts to play.

And to withdraw from life to practice austerities, to sit in a cave to meditate, does not necessarily mean spiritual advancement. It would not be right for the majority. Meher Baba seems to prefer us to be active and dynamic, though He wants us to accept whatever experience is necessary for our spiritual progress and development.

Meher Baba helps us in so many ways not to worry or fear and to develop this right attitude toward life. It sounds so simple yet most of us find it so difficult. "Don't worry," says Baba to someone and usually if that person is receptive he soon begins to realize what a worrier he is, even though it may have been in the depths of his subconscious self; and the measure of the new inrush of life that fills him is the measure of Baba's help.

It is a subtle and pernicious foe that we have to fight; but if we follow Baba's advice we soon find that troubles and fears begin to vanish, because the things that were important to us before do not matter anymore. Why should we worry when we can turn to Him and love Him and serve Him? We must try to know and understand ourselves truly; for Meher Baba says:

> Everything is within you: the secret of
> Life...God.

We are part of all; it is the veils of illusion that prevent our seeing clearly. We have gradually to shed these veils; to lose our ego, to die to the lower self; and we will awaken like a dreamer from sleep.

Sometimes Baba, in order to help us, brings our faults up to the boiling point. The person who worries, worries more than ever. A climax comes, an emotional upheaval takes place within the person. Then if they have the courage to face up to themselves, and to realize the fault lies within themselves, in a flash the whole thing clears up and they are free from that particular worry. If they lack courage or have not enough love or faith to trust Baba, then they perhaps turn against Him or blame Him for their own weaknesses.

Meher Baba is always there, waiting, ready to guide and teach us; whatever our weaknesses or worries, we can go to Him. And with patient love He will help us again and again.

Meher Baba's telling us not to worry has an added significance at the moment, for we are living in thrilling and trying times. The approaching spiritual age calls for our recognition of the verity of the brotherhood of man. All our resources and powers of endurance will be taxed in the struggle. Out of chaos, order comes. Meher Baba stands like a beacon, beckoning us on. He shows us by His example the heights we can reach; with perfect poise and equilibrium He walks the earth. His Love is our inspiration, and if there are dark days and all goes from us, we need not worry or despair.

Might He not be saying, as Francis Thompson says in *The Hound of Heaven*:

All which I took from thee
I did but take not for thy harms
But just that thou mightest seek it in My
   arms
All which thy child's mistake
Fancies is lost, I have stored up for thee at
   home
Rise, clasp My hands and come.

               —Meher Baba Journal
               April 1940

LOVE THAT NEVER TIRES

 In July 1939 I, along with Margaret and Ena Child, who played piano for her, went on holiday to St. Tropez to a cottage we had rented from Rosmond Wise. At first we had a lovely time but then the weather changed, there was an announcement that Russia and Germany had signed a pact, and then a cable arrived from my mother: "Return, brothers called up!" We knew this meant war, so of course we returned as quickly as we could.

Baba had told Margaret and me to go to India if war broke out, so when I got back from France, I arranged to come up from Hindhead and go to the Home Office with her to get visas to travel. But only those going abroad on urgent business or for special reasons were being given permits to leave the country. I had no valid reason. Margaret, however, was lucky. She had been acting as guardian to Rustom's son, Falu, who was in England at school. She told the Home Office that he could not travel back to India alone, so she was given permission to accompany him.

I was terribly upset and cabled Baba. He replied that I was not to worry and that I was where He wanted me to be. I had no idea until years after the war that the day I went up to London my brother-in-law cabled Baba behind my back, saying my mother needed me to look after her. Ironically only two years later I left Hindhead for war work in London and never lived with my mother again, although our relationship was always to remain close and loving.

Margaret and I had become very close at Nasik and, although we promised to write to each other as often as we could, I missed her very much when she had gone to India. I wrote Baba that I felt alone and asked Him what war work I should do. He replied, "Only obey the laws of your country." An undated letter from Him also helped:

The Links, Bangalore

Yes, you are right, I have not written to you for a long time....

You speak truly and from deep experience when you say you can only learn through suffering and experience. Do you know these lines of Hafiz?

He who would tread my path, the thorn of
grief will find
What pilgrim hath in fear of this, his quest
resigned
Thou knowest well, he who attains true
perfect love
Is he upon whose Soul grief as a lamp hath
shin'd.

It is the "ego" which is the cause of this temporary suffering, but it is also the means to eternal happiness and bliss, but believe Me when I say that the real happiness which lies in store for you is well worth the present suffering and struggle. The greater the capacity to love the greater the pangs of separation. These pangs of separation are felt, not only by those living physically apart from the Beloved, but equally by those living near; in fact, the feeling of separation is greatly intensified when living close physically and while not having the conscious experience of union and oneness... Love—work and obey Me—each of you.

My work just now is heavy, apart from the universal work for the upliftment of all. I have the work for the center which entails much work and time, every detail of which I supervise personally, although allotting to each the particular side of the work to which each is suited. It is to be on a very large scale consisting of many different sections but all under one guidance! You will read about it all in the magazine. . . .

M. S. IRANI

Baba was referring to the Universal Spiritual Center in Bangalore, Mysore (Byramangala), the foundation stone of which was laid on December 17, 1939. Ultimately this center was never built, but a great deal of work and preparation went into it.

I had now completed my two articles and had sent them to India for the *Meher Baba Journal.* The second was called "*A Love that Never Tires:*"

For a Love that never tires?
O heart, are you great enough for Love?
I have heard of thorns and briars.

—*Tennyson*

All Saints, Mystics, and Lovers of God know these thorns and briars, for the path they tread, bears them as a signpost. Once started, travelers on that path cannot, even if they would, turn back, for they are consumed ceaselessly with the love and desire for the Divine, it is a nostalgia or a glimpse that haunts them, and drives them ever on in more Love for the Beloved. If the end be a martyrdom or an ecstasy, both are the same, for they go with the Beloved's name on their lips, and a *certainty of knowing* that no cruelty of the world can take away.

So went St. Joan of Arc to the stake, rather than deny her Voices; so was Mansur Hallaj crucified by the ignorant masses, because he would not retract his declaration that he was God. So St. Francis of Assisi turned away from a life of sin, consumed with love for Jesus, and humbly and willingly endured hardships and poverty embracing the lepers, hailing all as his brethren, even "Brother Sun" and "Sister Moon" for everywhere was the face of his Beloved, Jesus. So, Akhenaton, the God-intoxicated Pharaoh of Egypt, struggling against the worn-out creeds of a corrupt priesthood, sang the praises of the One God, in words that show the strength and truth of his Vision.

What is this divine fever that through the ages has

moved countless men and women to renounce joyfully all the things that the rest of mankind hold so dear? Possessions, fame, security, family, in fact everything that the majority spend their lives and energies accumulating. Wordsworth glimpsed something of the Truth when he said:

> Not in entire forgetfulness
> And not in utter nakedness
> But trailing clouds of glory do we come
> From God Who is our home.*

At the first stirrings within of this Divine Consciousness, we are filled with the longing to return from whence we came; coming *unconsciously*, we must go back *consciously*. That is the great drama and struggle. God, the Infinite, through us, attains full consciousness of Himself. As drops from that Divine Ocean, we must go through the evolutionary process, from the lowest forms, until as man we attain full consciousness; but as it is the destiny of man to attain God-consciousness (which is the consciousness of his Real Self). Through the process of reincarnation, he takes different earthly forms to gain the necessary experience for this full development; when he desires the Divine, he takes the first step on the upward path.

In mystic language, the path is likened to a razor's edge, as the Lover must endure trials and hardships.

Intimations of Immortality—Wordsworth

Maya (illusion) tries to hold him back, but he learns that it is through the unreal that he must come to the Real. Now, he knows the Goal and nothing can hold him back. It is for him, as Hafiz, the great Persian Mystic, said:

> He who would tread my Path, the thorn of
>   grief will find
> What pilgrim hath in fear of this, his quest
>   resigned.
> Thou knowest well, he who attains true
>   perfect love
> Is he upon whose soul, grief as a lamp, has
>   shined.

Also in the words of the Spanish mystic, Ramon Llull:

> Pensively, the lover trod those paths that
> lead to the Beloved. Now he stumbled and
> fell amongst thorns, but they were to him as
> flowers and as a bed of love.

By himself, man can go a great part of the way, but for the final and blissful Liberation, he must contact a Perfect Master. It is for this reason that Masters take human form, to help others to reach the consciousness that they have attained.

We are told that there are always a certain number of Masters in the world, but they live and work apart from and unknown to the general public. It is only at certain periods known as *Avataric* or Messianic, when civilization has again reached material heights but spiritually is at a low level that One comes into the open and declares—shows Himself—as the *Avatar* (Messiah) in order to give a spiritual push to the whole of humanity. He is called in different ages by different titles, but His mission is always the same, to show the world, according to the capacity of the period, by His example, how life should be lived. He attracts by Love alone, and to follow Him, the heart must indeed "be great enough for Love." His is not an easy way but those who love Him, in any age, know that it is the only way, for He awakens Love in them; they are changed in the twinkling of an eye. They know that they must follow His path, do His bidding, and endure to the end, with full acceptance of the "thorns and briars." They bear witness to His Truth, and though in the world and at the service of the world, they are not of it.

Thus man becomes God, as God becomes man. It is for our sakes He comes and limits Himself to the sorrows and sufferings of Man, and by so doing He shows us His Divine Love, and the meaning of life in all its mystery and fullness.

The most materially minded amongst us must admit that today we have need of such a "One" to walk and talk with us, to show us anew the way; otherwise where are we going? All around us the world is shaking. Nations are at war, persecutions and horrible crimes are committed on defenseless peoples. Beneath our feet, the things we have valued and accumulated are crumbling; ideas and standards are changing and shifting; everything seems chaotic.

What must we understand by these signs? As of old, those who have been watching and waiting, know. The star has appeared in the east. The signs are manifold. The world not knowing, but rent and torn sends up a cry. "The Man is needed!"—"The God-Man!" who will once again show us the meaning of a life of Love. Only such a One, who comes with authority, can show us what is real and what is unreal, can *awaken us* to the Brotherhood of Man.

We who have already been privileged to contact Shri Meher Baba, feel that it is He who will be the awakener of Humanity for this age. He is of the stature of Christ; His overwhelming Love, His humanity inspires and will inspire, all who come to Him. His disciples come from all countries, are of all colors, religions, and castes. He works to unite the East and West in love and harmony, so that they will balance and reinforce each other. This is His Mission. He Himself combines all qualities that can be acceptable to all men, all races to the farthest ends of the earth. His call is clear and insistent, for it is the call of the Divine within us all. His is the Love that never tires, but we have to rise to the greatness of that Love.

Delia DeLeon
London

I was glad to hear that my literary efforts were well received. A letter came from Baba dated February 10, 1940:

The Links, Bangalore

Dearest Leyla,

I was indeed happy to receive, on the same day, two letters from you and also your two articles for the magazine, which I know were written for Me and came straight from the heart. I like both and especially the one on Love.

When you feel this urge to express yourself on paper, never check it. As you try to put these thoughts down they will become clearer and give you a deep understanding. Much that is within is often in such a chaotic state that to separate one idea from another is not easy.

I know you better than you know yourself and I will teach you in My own way all the things concerning your Real Self. Seek and strive to know Me—your Beloved—and bit by bit you will know your Real Self, *for am I not your real self.*

Realize Me and you will know God. No other pursuit is worthwhile when you have met the Beloved. Everything then centers around Him. You see all beauty through Him be it expressed through poetry, art, or music, or through life itself. All work whether of your hands or academic is done for Him and your only attachment is your Beloved. All service then becomes selfless whether done for friend, family, or stranger. All are one and toward this "One" the motive too is one—to please Him, *whom to please is to know.* There is no other knowing. Feeling is not knowing.

To please Me is *to do*, but doing what? That which

your Beloved commands you. This is My way, My path. "My yoke is easy and My burden is light." My way with you all is the shortest way to Union which I long for infinitely more than you can ever long. Although the game is of My own making, still I must suffer to enjoy the game of realizing Myself consciously in all creation. But it is up to you, My beloved ones, who know Me in the flesh as none other can, to lessen this suffering and give Me all the happiness you are capable of. Will you do this for Me? Help Me in thought, word, and action. Let your thoughts be always of Me—your work spring always from love, and your action be expressive of one who seeks in all she does to please Him who is ever present in the heart of His Beloved Leyla. This thought will give you eternal happiness and bliss in the midst of the sad times through which the world is now passing and must face up to. The suffering of all will be terrible, but remember that underneath are the "Everlasting Arms" to keep you happy in your faith and love to the very end. I will never fail you and will never leave you.

I am writing shortly to Minta. My love and blessings to your dear mother and to all your family.

All My love to dearest Leyla.

M. S. IRANI

Needless to say this wonderful letter was a comfort and inspiration to all during the war. As was the first part of this poem by Minnie Louise Hoskins, read by King George IV in his Christmas message of 1939. I sent it to India and was amused to hear in later years that Margaret had the task of reading it out every

Christmas at Myrtle Beach.

> I said to the man who stood at the gate of the year,
> Give me a light that I may tread safely into the
> unknown.
> And he replied, "Go out into the darkness and
> put your hand into the hand of God.
> That will be to you better than light and safer
> than a known way!"
> So I went forth and finding the Hand of God, trod
> gladly into the night.
> And He led me toward the hills and the breaking
> of day in the lone East.

The Links, Bangalore
March 14, 1940

Dearest Leyla,

Since last I wrote, which was not more than three
weeks back, many changes in plans have taken place. In
short, we all leave here, with the exception of the *mast*
and some of the *mandali*, on April 1st. We shall be six
weeks on the way, stopping at various places, the last
being Panchgani where we spent the summer two years
ago. We arrive back in Meherabad on 14th May, just
when the monsoon breaks. Goa and Gersappa Falls are
the two best known places at which we shall stop a few
days respectively, but for the other stopping places they
will be either at small villages or by the sea or in the
mountains. On this tour I am avoiding all cities. The
last tour we stopped mostly in cities. Margaret will be

with us for the trip, as even if she does go to Australia to examine students she will not leave before the end of June. I want her with us on the tour.

I will see you are kept informed of all our movements and do not have to complain that you hear no news for weeks on end! Margaret and Kitty are entirely to blame and I will "tick both off very severely." Lack of time certainly cannot be the excuse. Perhaps Margaret writes that she is "walked off her feet" with work!

All My Love, dearest Leyla.

M. S. IRANI

Be writing as usual and pass on the news to others of the group.

In 1940 Will and I were asked by Baba to print and distribute 20,000 booklets. We were to be jointly responsible for paying for and distributing them. This, of course, we did—all in the middle of a forty-day fast. I did not know how I was going to find the money but I accepted and followed Baba's request without hesitation. Then an unexpected gift from abroad enabled me to pay my share of the costs. This taught me that when you do something whole-heartedly for Baba, against all the odds, the way will open out and it will be successful; but if you hesitate and worry about the results, it is never so easy.

This was the first time Baba asked me to work with Will Backett, an association which was to last until his death. It was never easy for us to work together as we were poles apart; I, with my theatrical background, was very happy-go-lucky and Will, a Methodist, was rather prim and proper. On the other hand, I always got on well with Mary, who had a great sense of fun.

So the time passed by at Hindhead. I joined the Red Cross and worked on a farm belonging to Lloyd George. Then early in 1942, I decided to go to London and get a proper war job before being called up. I cabled Baba and asked Him to help me. He replied, "What you feel alright will have my internal help."

I was terribly lucky and landed a most unusual job as supervisor at the Florence Nightingale Hospital, which was being used as a hostel for people who had lost their homes through the bombing. There we would provide food and clothes and allocate rooms.

The hospital was centrally located and easy for people to visit and I was able to hold Baba meetings there. Christmas Humphreys, president of the Buddhist Society, came and spoke for me; Tom Sharpley was working for me there; and, of course, Charles and Will came regularly to see me, so it became quite a Baba center.

Many new people came to these meetings; Dorothy Hopkinson, at that time married to the author Hugh Kingsmill, came to see me often. She had dreamt of Baba and recognized His picture in Charles Purdom's book, *The Perfect Master*. She was interested in dream interpretation and we had many interesting conversations, but it was with Minta she became very close.

After 1940 Baba did not send dictated and signed letters because Chanji, the letter writer and Baba's devoted secretary, died during the war while on a visit to Kashmir. Dear Chanji, he seemed so akin to us and all Kimco loved him as an uncle.

Margaret and I kept our promise to each other to keep in touch and I depended on her for news of Baba's doings in India. Any clothes I could spare I sent over there but, while life was difficult for those in India, for us in the midst of war and death it was also full of problems. However, I liked my job and lived fully each day and I felt I developed and matured a great deal during this period. In particular I was happy that there was somewhere where anyone who wished to could come and hear about Baba.

In 1941 another article of mine appeared in the *Meher Baba Journal:*

THOUGHTS ON CHRISTMAS DAY

This is Xmas day—the third one of the war which is now worldwide, for all people have to be stirred in suffering to be ready for the spiritual awakening. Already we can see the pattern taking shape and we await Baba's day and hour with faith, love, and fortitude.

A large portrait of Him stands in my room and I have decorated it with holly—a poignant reminder of that divine manifestation of love which took place 2,000 years ago. Now, the Christ is again with us, but few know Him or love Him as yet—all they know is that something big is at work which has shattered the old world and is reshaping everyone and everything for the new world order, not the order envisaged by warlords, but one of Divine Love and spiritual aspiration.

"And the Word was made flesh and dwelt among us . . . full of grace and truth." These words trail through my mind and as I write them, Baba's love flows through me, in me, and all around me and I see His face so beautiful, holy, and full of truth. So, if our blood and suffering and tears lead us a fraction more toward Him, how worthwhile, for it teaches us to see with spiritual clarity and to distinguish the real from the unreal. We can say with the Upanishads—

> From the unreal, lead me to the Real.
> From darkness, lead me to Light
> From death, lead me to Immortality.

If we look, we can find Him at the center and core of our being, and when we have found Him, we know there is no other. If we let Him, He will teach us, guide us, and show us how to live more fully and truly.

It is the reason and purpose of our lives to find the Divine within us and to merge with that Divinity. Baba, being one with the source of all, is in us all and stands to us as a pattern, a focal point, and inspiration. To see Him is to see all beauty and all imagined beauty. To know Him is joy beyond measure. To work for Him and do His bidding is to gain a fuller experience of His wisdom and power. The impossible becomes the possible and ways and means open up to fulfill His orders in interesting and unusual ways. These last few months have shown this to me so clearly that I wish, on the Xmas day, to rededicate myself to Baba in love, and faith, and service. I did this instantly ten years ago but now, with fuller knowledge of His selfless work for humanity, I feel it is the greatest privilege any of us can have to serve Him and help in any little way.

Through the distribution of His booklets in India, America, and the British Isles, many more thousands of people have heard of Him and His work, and felt drawn to Him in love. Baba entrusted this work of printing and distributing at least 20,000 booklets to Mr. William Backett and myself, and we have been helped by many devoted and enthusiastic followers and friends as well as by strangers who have made their first contact with Baba through the booklet. Some who met Baba ten years ago, or heard of Him then and were not drawn to Him, have now responded amazingly, and wonderful work has been done by all in the distribution, and by personal explanations, when an opportunity offered.

In addition, the booklets have gone as far afield as Canada, West Indies, Central America, South Africa, and Australia. It has been an illuminating experience for all concerned. When the order came from Baba to print and distribute at least 20,000 copies, there seemed no possibility of raising the money and war conditions had to be surmounted; but it was amazing how things worked out—a loan made it possible to put the work in hand without any delay and step by step all obstacles disappeared. We managed to get the amount of money we needed—gifts came in small and large amounts and, later on, unexpected help from abroad enabled us to pay back the loan. All rallied round to the best of their ability and this cooperation had made it possible to distribute by Xmas over 20,000 booklets and has brought confirmation of Baba's promise and message in which He sent His blessings to all those who participate in this great work and help to carry out His instructions satisfactorily.

Now the King is about to give His Message, over the wireless, to the Empire. We await the day when the

King of Kings will give His Divine Message to all
humanity.

—*Meher Baba Journal*

It is sad that it takes a war to bring out qualities of bravery,
self-sacrifice, and discipline in people. It seems to teach us to live in
the moment, nothing material seems to matter when everything
you owned could be destroyed in a moment. In fact, Margaret lost
most of her material possessions when a bomb destroyed the
warehouse where they were being stored while she was in India.
There was no point in worrying—we were all linked together for
the common aim. I felt Baba was with me, directing and teaching
me all the time.

"GO PANAMA"

So the war years went by and I and my family and most of my friends came through the war unscathed. Only dear Christine was killed but I am sure Baba was with her at the last. Before I even realized it I was welcoming Margaret back to England and hearing first hand about all those years in India and all the changes. I could hardly believe the story of the mad dog which bit her and of her extraordinary experience thinking perhaps she would develop hydrophobia—although no one else seemed concerned, not even Baba. This at a time when madness was being released in the West, first in the concentration camps and then in the World War. Margaret, being Western, might have been used by Baba to absorb this special brand of suffering.

There was also the strange story of the cat, which Margaret relates later in her book, *The Dance of Love*:

> Someone sent Baba a beautiful Siamese cat. The
> animal had had a strange upbringing. It lived in a

three-room cage. A place to eat, a place to sleep, and a place for toilet purposes, and she did not want to come out and face the world. Baba had the cage brought into my small room—it practically filled the floor space—with orders to me to train the cat to come out and run around in the usual way of cats. It took me some weeks, but in the end "Geisha," as she had been named, would let me take her out on the hills and from there she would return to her room.

One evening—the first night of the monsoons—the skies seemed to open and release something like Niagara Falls into Meherabad and the country round about. It was difficult to hear anything else. Early in the evening Baba opened the door of my room, came in, and made signs that I should put the cat outside in the yard. It was seldom—after all Baba's training—that I made any protests, but this time I pointed out to Baba that it would be hard on the animal to throw it out on such a night. Baba gave in to me. The next evening, however, the same thing occurred. Again I started to argue. This time, however, Baba, who had never shown me power, only love, seemed to shoot up to about seven feet high, sending a wave of power toward me, and spelled on the board, "Is this My cat or yours?" I could only say, "Yours, Baba," and hurriedly seizing the cat, took it to the door and threw it out into a dark bath of descending water. Cat lovers may be pleased to hear that Geisha found a hole in the kitchen wall and spent a comfortable night out of the deluge.

This happened at the time of the Normandy invasion when bad weather on the first night made the crossing of the Channel impossible. On the second night, however, Churchill ordered the invasion to go ahead in spite of the weather and I think Margaret's story might show why Britain was specially protected at this time.

With the end of the war my job finished. I had no home to go to and did not know what to do. I started negotiations for a property which had a small theater and which we all thought would be suitable for a Baba center, but at the last moment it fell through. It was strange that my second attempt to start a center for Baba failed, so evidently that was not my work. Simultaneously came an offer from an aunt to visit Panama. I cabled Baba and He replied, "Go Panama."

I stopped off in New York on the way in February 1947 and stayed with a cousin but, of course, got in touch with Elizabeth Patterson, who had a lovely home there and she invited me to stay the weekend. It was wonderful to see her again and hear all her news. Sadly I was not able to see Norina as she was quite ill, but I did make the acquaintance of Filis Frederick and Adele Wolkin, who were helping to look after her.

By this time Margaret was also living and working in New York and I was pleased to see her. She looked so well and happy in her work with the American Ballet Theatre and from that time she made her life in America. Baba told her always to teach, which she did until retirement in 1986, and through it brought a wonderful group of young dancers to Him. She died at 97 in February 1990 in Myrtle Beach.

Stopping off in Jamaica to see my sister for a while, I went on to Panama, where I soon started weekly meetings with my cousin, Walter, who had met Baba at East Challacombe in 1932 and still felt a link with Him. I gave several talks on Baba and of the people who came, Mrs. Otelia Tejeira, the Panamanian representative at UNESCO, became very interested.

Of course, I felt cut off from things in India, but I had become close to Elizabeth this time in New York and she was now staying with Baba at Pimpalgaon (Meherazad). In December 1947 I received this very newsy letter from her which gave me a lovely picture of what life was like with Baba in India and made me feel closer to them.

Dear Delia,

Baba had told me that you have written that you feel cut off and have received no letter from here in a long time. Indeed I know how you feel; and as I feel so privileged to be here I shall try to keep you more regularly informed. At the same time, I have sent word over to Kitty to write you, knowing that anything she would say would be quite different, as she and Rano are staying in Meherabad and Norina and I are at Pimpalgaon. We can only communicate, by order, to one another through Mani writing to Naja; otherwise no chit-chat letters permitted. The note from Mani is then given to the man who delivers the milk from Meherabad here by bicycle; and twice a day going back and forth is 64 miles bicycling a day—just to impress you!

Baba has been on a number of *mast* trips to the north, the last one to Mount Abu. All along the route were refugees and evacuees, an unbelievable number at that time. Yet consciously or unconsciously they came in contact with Baba. Without their sufferings and struggles, would they have ever come in His spiritual atmosphere and contact?

On December 5th, Baba went up the nearby mountain, Mt. Tembi*, where a hut has been built for Him on the summit and another a little lower down for some of His _mandali_. It is a very beautiful spot and at the top a single ridge. It was very difficult to dig deep enough for the four corner poles of the hut, as it is so rocky. We all walked up with Baba to the summit, about three hundred feet above where we are staying. Then He went into seclusion. Baba says He has "special work to finish." He will not be there more than ten days at this time. It is a seclusion and not a fast; all the food for four persons is carried up there (after being cooked here) in tiffin boxes. Also water is carried up. So we see a lot of coming and going, but of course everything is taken to the _mandali_, not to Baba Himself.

The Nagar _mast_, that is the sixth plane _mast_ of Ahmednagar, is up there, too. He is an old man and they carried him up in a chair. Baba works with him six hours a day, I understand.

Mrs. Duce and her daughter, Charmian, are flying to India to see Baba shortly... Mrs. Duce is a Sufi leader and wants to meet Baba. She has heard of Him through Norina and myself and Rabia Martin in San Francisco. Now that Rabia died, Ivy Duce is her Sufi successor.

Mrs. Duce met Meherjee several times in the United

*Now known as Seclusion Hill.

States. When she comes, Baba says she can stay here a week. Dr. Ghani will be called from Lonavla to talk with her as he has Sufi background, and also to confer with Dr. Donkin about the *mast* book (*The Wayfarers*) they are writing concerning Baba's work with *masts* since Rahuri period. It will be quite a large book eventually, on a little-known subject.

Now to return to Mrs. Duce and her daughter, they will occupy Norina's room and Norina will have to move to the girls' house close by. Moving is easy but where to put your baggage is another thing when you "live in boxes" as we do here. Another item is that there are four dogs now, all of which do not get on with each other. Cracker is Mani's Scottie and being in the group first, thinks he has priority. He definitely does not get on with Foundy, because Cracker is jealous and Foundy can't see enough to protect himself; however, that does not make too much concern because Foundy spends his time under my bed. He is beginning to show his age considerably.

Then there is Daney, a Great Dane puppy which Baba gave me. He is about five months old and a huge "baby." Cracker and he are taken out together for walks and rough-housing with each other by two Hindu local boys, one with a pink turban and the other with a yellow turban—they look as if they were going to a dog race when one sees them start out. Daney is friends with Foundy and also sleeps in my room at night—so we are three "personalities" in one enclosure.

To keep us still busier, a fourth dog, a darling soft

small dachshund, arrived through Sarosh. An English captain and his wife who returned to England gave it, with all its pedigrees, to Him. The six-month quarantine law in England is so heart-rending to those who return. Mani had wanted a dachshund before she had Cracker and Sarosh had heard about it. However, now that Cracker is such a firework, she could not have another dog right there. Of course, I came along just as it was being returned to the car and it gave me one look which melted my heart (easy to be melted by animals), and I said, like the expectant mother, "It is as easy to have three children as two." However, Norina returned from a walk and fell unexpectedly in love with "Banja" (his full name is Banjamore); he now is in her room adjoining mine. The first day Daney, who is so huge, barked his head off and we thought it was because he wanted to gobble up the little "dachs" and then, fortunately, we found that it was merely the ball that the dachs played with!

Well, now the "unresolved question" is what to do with these darlings when there are visitors. Norina says that Mrs. Duce, being a Sufi, will want to meditate and expect only peace and quiet in an ashram! Of course, with Baba there is a place for everything....

You ask "Baba's plans," yet we do not know any or much more than you who are not here. I do believe that Baba is going to America, because He has said it, yet "when" is in His own good time. One day we think we can see signs of His probable departure on the horizon, and the next day the horizon looks as if He were staying here for next year. But don't be influenced by anything "I don't know" because Baba is so fluid in His movements—it could be any time after January.

I am afraid that if you return to England now your plans will not be "fluid" and you will be there "indefinitely." If you want to be ready to join Baba when and wherever, then as He says, "remain in Panama or Jamaica." I am sure time will bear this out clearly to you....

Baba sent His Blessings to your group. Did you get it? And eternal love to you.

I have sent you, and also to Margaret, a photo of Baba for Christmas, but it may get there after Christmas. If others like it, you might have it copied in smaller size. I sent one to Will in England, too, and Phyllis (Filis) for the New York group. It helps to have a new photo of our Beloved.

Well, please keep me in touch with you, too.

Keep your good health and spirits and know that anything can happen at any time and you may be with Him again "anywhere at His choosing!"

Love, in which Norina joins me.

Elizabeth

Needless to say, this letter cheered me up immensely, helping me not to feel too detached and isolated in Panama. And, too, Panama has great geographical importance linking by canal as it does the Atlantic and Pacific and the two parts of America. There is also a strong American influence either side of the Canal and I am quite certain that the reason Baba sent me there was to make links for Him.

RETURN TO INDIA

I had been in Panama a year and three months, when a cable came from Baba inviting me to go to India. Of course, I was overjoyed and cabled Baba immediately that I was coming. I also received a letter from Jean Schloss, who by this time was divorced from Malcolm and calling herself Jean Adriel. She told me she was going to India, too, and could we arrange to travel together? I flew back to New York to meet her and by an almost miraculous feat managed to obtain passage, first from America to England, and then traveled with Jean from England on one of the already overcrowded ships sailing to India.

All Baba's disciples had been asked to observe some special discipline from June 2 to July 20, 1948 and He had sent out a list of options to choose from. When Jean and I sailed on the Anchor line from England on June 26, we had decided to observe the option of a semi-fast—eating only one meal a day, with tea or coffee once— which seemed to be the most practical selection for a period of travel.

During the voyage we had many interesting talks and speculated about the future. Neither of us had seen Baba since we said goodbye to Him in Cannes in 1937, and we both felt that deep changes had taken place in our inner selves. We had both been through material and emotional upheavals. I had experienced the dark days of war with all that they implied and I could well see why Baba had left me in the active world to be plunged deeper into duality and the illusions of *maya*—it was psychologically what my character needed. Jean had written her book, *Avatar*, and had been instrumental in establishing the center, Meher Mount, in California. We both felt the moment was ripe for starting a new phase.

Before landing in India, the boat stopped in Pakistan for one day where we were met by Minoo Kharas and shown around, Jean being treated as rather a celebrity because of her book. And then, with feelings of great joy, for we knew we were soon to see our Beloved, we watched the lights of Bombay come into view. We landed the next morning, July 15, and were met on the dock by four disciples.

We had expected to go straight to Baba but He had sent instructions that we were to spend four days in Bombay and then go to Ahmednagar and stay at Meherabad. Meherazad was not ready as it was still in the process of being renovated and enlarged. We were not to see Baba, although He was in Ahmednagar, until August 10, when the building at Meherazad would be completed and we could go to stay with Him there. Of course, we were bitterly disappointed; we had been asked for three months, and it looked as if a month would elapse before actually seeing Baba—this was our first little test.

Our host and hostess in Bombay were Homai and Meherjee

Karkaria, two charming Persian disciples. They and others gave us a warm-hearted welcome and did everything possible to make our stay pleasant. We met many old friends and heard their experiences over the years and found most people inclined to agree with us that Baba, in this new impersonal phase, was trying to push His disciples away, forcing them to stand on their own two feet without His outward aid.

Everyone was observing the disciplines ordered by Baba, most of them fasting. One group of four women had opted to say the Divine Name aloud one million times a day. We thought this a complete impossibility, but the first day it took them fifteen hours and after that ten hours. At the end of the first week, Baba ordered them to stop and keep silence for the second week; the third week they were to feed a different poor person every day; and the fourth week they were to fast. During this time one of the women, Dinah, became unconscious and one of the other women, a doctor, diagnosed signs of death—the eyes turned up, no heart beat. In alarm, the women called on Baba and suddenly Dinah awoke wondering what was happening. She said she had felt a deep inner peace and ecstatic calm.

Then the message came that Jean and I were to go to Meherabad. We left Bombay on the evening of July 18, changing trains at 3:30 in the morning. The stations we passed through were swarming with refugees, living where they could in the most pitiable conditions of poverty and dirt. This was the aftermath of freedom from Britain and partition in which Pakistan was created as a separate Moslem state—apparently more people were killed in the region during this period than during World War II.

We arrived in Ahmednagar at 9 a.m. and were met by Adi Sr. and Kaka, who were surprised that we had brought so much luggage. But we explained we had come prepared for any change in plans—our stay might just as easily be three years as three months. We drove up the hill at Meherabad, passing the men's quarters down below. Kitty greeted us at the gate and we met the other women who were living there, including Norina, Elizabeth, and Katy Irani. Kitty gave us a note from Baba that said He had decided to see us sooner than originally planned. He would come to Meherabad on July 23 and we, along with Norina and Elizabeth, would go with Him to the new center, Meherazad, on August 20.

Meanwhile, we had four days to settle in at Meherabad. Baba has said that it was His first and last ashram. No one could stay there without becoming aware of the wonderful atmosphere of purity and serenity that pervades it. The house on the hill had been greatly extended since my last visit. Two large rooms had been built on top of the bungalow with steps leading up to them; and the garden was bigger, looking very green after the monsoon. There were two dogs and a peacock which fascinated us, especially when he strutted about with his magnificent tail fanned.

Baba had divided the women into four groups each with their own quarters and allowance. They were independent of each other but could mix if they chose. He explained that this was the best way of keeping the peace, as in this phase of His work He did not want to be troubled with their personal problems or personal ties as He was too busy with His universal *mast* work. The only women always allowed to be with Him at this time—except when He went on *mast* trips with the men—were Mehera, Mani, Meheru, and Dr. Goher. Kitty, Rano, and Naja were called from time to time.

During the war years life had been very austere, all had experienced suffering and hardship but now Baba was allowing them more freedom, but no luxuries. For the first time each group had its own little maid who was devoted to Baba and treated as a friend. Although all the water had to be heated, at that time it was in plentiful supply, as was the simple vegetarian food.

Jean and I were treated as guests and everyone was very kind and came offering help. The day after our arrival was the last day of the fast and we started regular meals with lunch at 11 a.m. and supper at 6 p.m. Our little maid, Valu, was charming. She came with us when we visited the cinema and came to listen every evening when we played the gramophone. She was quite a little actress: one night there was an uproar, Kitty and Katie thought a stray dog was mad, and Valu rushed up vividly talking and panto-miming the scene.

Then there was great excitement—a note arrived from Baba saying He was coming the next day to greet us. He had not paid the ashram a visit for more than a month, so the next morning the ashram was like a beehive from 5:30. Garlands of flowers were made, rooms were cleaned; everyone put on their best clothes. At last at 9 o'clock the car was heard coming up the hill.

Jean held a mauve garland and I a white as we lined up by the gate to greet Him. The car stopped and out climbed Mehera and Mani, but no Baba. Our hearts sank but smiling, they reassured us that He had only stopped off at the men's quarters for a little while. Sure enough the car went back down the hill and after five minutes Baba appeared at the gate. He held out His arms, a beaming smile on His face and we ran to embrace Him, the years falling away with all their problems and heartaches. After eleven long years it was absolute bliss when He hugged us; it was coming home again; time stood still—here was Reality! Only those who have had the felicity of being thus embraced can understand the extraordinary feeling of happiness it brings to be thus enfolded in Love.

He went to His room where, at the steps, Masi was waiting to perform the Hindu ceremony where a coconut is cracked at the Master's feet as a symbolic offering of the head and heart. Then Jean and I were told to follow Him into His room with Mehera and Mani. He said He was so happy to have us with Him. We were to stay at Meherabad for six weeks and during that time we were to rest, eat, not worry, and just think of Him because when we moved to Meherazad we would be kept busy all the time. He was going on a two-week *mast* tour, but for the six weeks we were at Meherazad, He would be with us all the time. He told us He was very, very tired with the weight of the Universe upon His shoulders, but soon that would change and so too would conditions in the West. He added, "Everyone is Baba, everything is Baba, and everywhere is Baba; and all else is zero."

He called the rest of the women in and jokingly asked me if I still liked eau de cologne, remembering that on my previous visit to India I was always using it because of the very hot weather. Then He walked around to inspect our quarters, saying, with the sweetness so characteristic of Him, that we were to have everything we really needed. He showed us the inside of the dome, where He was to be buried and where He had stayed seven months drinking only coffee, and then, after inspecting the rest of the ashram, He embraced us again before He left. We stood outside the gate to watch His car disappear.

Not having seen Him for so long we noticed quite a change: although physically He looked more powerful, He also looked much older, His hair was grayer and thinner, and He seemed to be suffering very much in spite of the power. His love and humor were still in evidence, but we felt that the emphasis now was on the impersonal aspect of God—except in rare instances, only Mehera was allowed to touch Him.

After this meeting, I felt calm and happy—I wrote at the time:

> A feeling of peace pervaded my being as if a benediction rested on my head. I knew it was right for me to be there at this moment but not before. I had just to be plunged more deeply into *maya* and come to terms with certain aspects of myself. Had not Baba written to me during the war: "You are nearer to Me where I want you than if you were near to Me physically where I did not want you. When we meet again, you will be a changed Leyla and yet the same."

> His time is always perfect, so that the dreaded house of nun-like seclusion on the hill now appears to be the perfect background to begin the new experience.

The next day Kitty took us down in the car to the men's quarters where Baba was seeing people for the first time in months. We drove up by Baba's little room where He stood garlanded, looking simply radiant. We went inside and He touched our cheeks and said how well we were looking.

Although the railway line runs right through the Meherabad property, trains do not usually stop, but at 9 o'clock that morning one stopped right outside for the first time. When the passengers, mostly from Poona and Jubbulpore, alighted they were allowed to see Baba but not to take His *darshan*. Half an hour later we were all summoned to the big hall and when Baba came in, everyone stood up and chanted, "Shri Sadguru Meher Baba, Ki Jai." He sat on a chair facing us and the seven names of God, written by Baba during the war, were sung: "Hari, Paramatman, Allah, Ahuramazda, God, Yezdan, Hu." Then a politician Baba had previously introduced to us stood up and made a speech hailing Baba as Avatar, some young girls sang a sacred song, and at 10:30 Baba stood up and closed the gathering.

While we were at Meherazad we chatted with the women and learned much of the history of the women's ashram and what had been happening during the war. Khorshed, Gulmai's niece, told us that at one time they had to chant the names of God, as given by Baba, for an hour every morning followed after a five-minute interval by one hour's meditation. Sometimes they were with Baba at the cinema by 5:30 in the morning, usually watching a three-hour program. At this period, she told us Baba found fault with everything and called them "second-hand furniture" and said, "Women can't keep quiet about anything, even when they are God-Realized." At another time He told them, "If you don't want to be old before your time, be cheerful in deed, word and thought, and in appearance—most of all in appearance. It is a divine art to look always cheerful, it helps others."

Mohammed, the *mast*, was still at Meherabad and we were told a story that at one time he kept demanding that Baba produce his wife. No one knew if, in fact, he had a wife but eventually to humor him Baba told him that he would see her that afternoon. He had one of the women of the village dress up to look like an awful old hag and presented her to Mohammed as his wife. This completely cured him of his desire to see her and he never referred to her again. Thus does Baba comply with our insistent desire, in order to make us free from that desire.

On the 29th, Jean and I had a joint interview with Baba. He asked us about everybody, Minta especially. I had brought with me a copy of the *Discourses* that Charles Purdom had been editing, with a view to publishing them in England under the title, *God to Man and Man to God*. Baba said He would call a meeting to discuss this later. He said He would take care of our health and gave me some vitamins (A, B, C, and D) to take on top of a prescription Dr. Nilu had given me.

In the following days I had three private interviews on alternate days. At the first of these Baba asked me to tell Him everything that had happened during the separation. I knew there was a reason in this recounting and so with streaming eyes I tried my best but, as always happens on these occasions, it doesn't seem necessary to say anything—one forgets anyway—the important thing is being in Baba's loving presence. However, I did manage to say that I was unhappy about the way I had been working for Him; I told Him I did not feel I adequately conveyed Him to others. He listened intently and gravely to all that I had to say, then spelled out on His board that from then on I would work for Him 100% to His satisfaction and my own peace of mind. He instructed me to write to several people giving them all His news and He told me that we were to leave in the middle of October for England, where I was to stay for two months before going on to Panama.

While at Meherabad, I was sharing a room with Jean, who had a passion for fresh air and kept the windows open all night so that the wind blew through the room. Consequently one morning I woke with a temperature. We were to meet Baba at 4:00 a.m. to go to the cinema to see Charlie Chaplin in "Gaslight" and Kitty told me Baba would be displeased if I did not make the effort to go, so I did. Baba was very sweet when he heard I was ill, said I should not have come, and allowed me to lie down; but at that time I did not tell Him why I was sick.

Then He went away on His *mast* tour as promised and we did not see Him again until another cinema visit on the 22nd. We continued our stay at Meherabad, even getting used to the early rising and retiring—part of the life of discipline. Then Baba called us to stay with Him at the house of a disciple in Ahmednagar until Meherazad was ready. Being so close to Him on a day-to-day basis we seemed to be lifted into a different vibration. All our thoughts and love and endeavors were focused on Baba. It was always an amazing and unforgettable experience to live like this. All time and space are there where He treads the earth.

Jean had taken the best bed as usual but Baba called me to Him and said Kitty had told Him what had happened and why I had been ill. He then said to me, "Why don't you fight her?" I was astonished and could only stutter, "How can I Baba, it would be so unpleasant?" So He said, "I will do it for you!" He went into our room and asked me to change beds with her, putting me in the best position. I am sure He did this to toughen me so that I would be prepared to fight when necessary as I was inclined to take the line of least resistance and give in.

We were all given jobs to do. One of mine was to read to Baba, at any hour He wished, from the thriller novels Margaret sent from the U.S. Sometimes He would start walking about, all around the house, and insisted that I walk behind Him still reading, much to the amusement of all. Every morning the newspaper was passed around and in the evenings when we all sat with Baba in the garden, He would ask us to tell Him the current world events and we would also have to tell jokes and funny stories.

At long last, Meherazad was ready and we moved to this

lovely new center. The villa resembled a Swiss chalet with Baba's quarters upstairs and the women on the ground floor. Facing this was a four-room bungalow occupied by Norina, Elizabeth, Jean, and myself, and all around was a beautiful garden supervised by Mehera. We had Western cooking sent over from the men's quarters, while Baba and the other women had Indian food cooked at the villa. It was very peaceful and wonderful in this lovely place with Baba and the girls—Rano and Dr. Goher were our only links with the outside world—there was a feeling of eternity and time-lessness and all thought of the outside world faded away.

When the day arrived for the official opening we put on our best clothes. Women from Meherabad, Ahmednagar, and other parts arrived and we had a meal sitting on cushions in the garden, then Kaka made a speech, relayed to us from the men's quarters, calling on all to love and serve Baba more and more. Baba opened the main door with a silver key and sat on a couch with Mehera by His side and was garlanded. Then Gulmai performed the arti ceremony.

There followed a period of intense activity as Baba had predicted. The promised meeting about Charles' edited version of the Discourses took place with Dr. Deshmukh who, for some reason, was opposed to their publication. After a lot of heated discussion, it was decided to drop the matter for the time being. Some time later, however, Deshmukh wrote to Charles and said he had changed his mind and the result was the book, God to Man and Man to God.

We were all very busy. Jean had special meditation to do every day and was also writing letters. I had to knock on her door at half time so that she could change over from one to the other without interruption. Norina was writing her memoirs while Elizabeth kept busy with business affairs and arranging for the formation of the Universal Spiritual League in America. It was proposed that we should form a similar one in England, with the American as the parent league. I was asked to write to the group in England and consult a solicitor about suitable rules.

I was also typing, very slowly, a book Dr. Ghani was working on, which turned out to be the first material of what was later collated and incorporated into Baba's book, *God Speaks*. And a curious episode occurred when Baba, saying He would like to visit Panama with His group, made me write off for booklets and information. When I received them I handed them to Baba and He put them in His pocket. The next day He handed them back to me and nothing more was said.

Much to Baba's disgust, Jean and I were ill alternately. He had, He said, planned several excursions and we must both get well so as not to miss them and we did manage to rally for the most important one: a delightful walk to Happy Valley where Baba said Rama and Sita had wandered in their exile and where we had, in fact, come on a picnic in 1936 while at the Nasik ashram. An event occurred on this outing which was very interesting: Baba put on Mehera's sandals; Mani put on Baba's; and Mehera was given Mani's to put on. Could this have presaged Mani assuming authority during Baba's periods of complete seclusion and the time when Mehera came more out of seclusion? On our way home there was a beautiful double rainbow in the sky—a symbol of hope and promise.

Every evening we would gather in the sitting room to be with Baba. We would read poems and Baba insisted on four of us telling funny stories. Luckily someone in America had sent a large book of jokes and so each morning the book was passed around and we each selected three or four and wrote them out ready for the evening—Norina used to say hers with great aplomb. While we were talking we often noticed a far away look on Baba's face, yet He always knew exactly what had been said.

I often read stanzas from Hafiz, Baba's favorite poet, and one evening I asked Mehera to ask Baba to let me read *The Hound of Heaven* by Francis Thompson. I started very nervously. It is a very long poem and as it went on and on I could see the looks of boredom on everyone's faces. Some time after this, I heard that when someone wanted to relate a long speech to Baba, which the *mandali* thought would be too wearing, Baba had said, "If I can stand Delia reading *The Hound of Heaven* I can stand anything."

When the sad day of our departure arrived, Baba said that we were not even to shed a tear, as we would be seeing Him again whatever happened. He told me if we could find a suitable house, He would come to England; so I was to go back to England for six weeks only, tell the group there all the plans, form the Spiritual League, and then go on to Panama and await His arrival. Jean was to go back to California. But we were both told that we would eventually return to India. We left in October, arriving in London in November 1948.

THE NEW LIFE

When I got back we held a meeting to form the Universal Spiritual League in Great Britain; Charles Purdom accepted the chairmanship. I was vice-chairman, and Will Backett, secretary and treasurer. Baba, of course, was president and He selected the other members of the committee, telling us not to throw it open for membership. This was the origin of the present Meher Baba Association and, strangely enough, although subsequently Baba resigned as president of other groups around the world, He did not resign from our group and is still the president today.

I left once more for Panama in February 1949 and immediately started making the arrangements for Baba's proposed visit. It was necessary to obtain visas and to find a suitable house where all could stay. All was going ahead swimmingly when a cable came telling me plans were changed—not an unusual occurrence with Baba—but this was a more dramatic change than ever before. The cable read: "Return England immediately starting New Life." Further instructions, I was told, awaited me there.

On my way back I met again many of the American group and Margaret, of course, but I also met up with Kim, who with Margaret's encouragement had written to Baba asking Him to take her back and she was now holding *Discourses* sessions in her New York flat. After a short time she again lost touch with me but when she returned to England in 1969 she contacted me and we now keep in touch for Christmas and birthdays.

I must admit I felt rather sheepish when I arrived back in London, but my family took it very well. They must have been getting used to it by now and as usual I did manage to see the funny side. The Baba group learned from letters that we had to cancel all plans and that we might never see Baba again:

Baba ends His old life of cherished hopes and multifarious activities and with a few companions begins His NEW LIFE of complete renunciation and absolute hopelessness from 16th October 1949. Although Baba's and His companions' New Life will be known to everyone, and their whereabouts will be no secret, no one should try to see Baba or His companions for any reason whatsoever, as Baba will not see anyone of them, nor allow His companions to do so.

No one should try to communicate with Baba or His companions under any circumstances, or for any reason whatsoever.

By Order of Baba

We arranged a meeting to discuss a long circular sent out by Baba. From what we gleaned, the New Life was to be a most extraordinary period—a period of "hopelessness and helplessness." The centers at Meherabad and Meherazad were disbanded and all property sold. Baba and His companions were to wander around India, at times begging for their food. We had been planning to open a center in London and we discussed scrapping this idea as Baba had told us to cancel all plans, but Will had already found a suitable property in Ealing and he was committed to buying it. So he and Mary sold their house in Sevenoaks and moved to London. I felt this was mainly to afford an opportunity for them to live in a more central place where they could do more active work for Baba and eventually they sold this house in Ealing as well and moved to a small bungalow in Acton which became a mecca for Baba lovers and visitors from abroad. This, I am sure, was what Baba wanted.

In a strange way having been through the war I sensed something of the meaning of the New Life, except that the war was thrust upon us and the New Life was Baba's personal choice. It was a hard period but we carried on—it was to be Old Life-New Life and then Life. In 1950, Baba went into seclusion for a phase of the New Life He called "*Manonash*" (annihilation of the mind), and afterward He issued this very moving statement:

> To try to understand with the mind that which the mind can never understand, is futile; and to try to express by sounds of language and in forms of words the transcendent state of the soul, is even more futile.
>
> All that can be said, and has been said, and will be said by those who live and experience that state, is that when the false self is lost, the Real Self is found; that the birth of the Real can follow only the death of the false; and that dying to ourselves—the true death which ends

all dying—is the only way to perpetual life. This means that when the mind with its desires, cravings, and longings, is completely consumed by the fire of Divine Love, then the infinite, indestructible, indivisible, eternal Self is manifested. This is *manonash*, the annihilation of the false, limited, miserable, ignorant, destructible "I," to be replaced by the real "I," the eternal possessor of Infinite Knowledge, Love, Power, Peace, Bliss, and Glory in its unchangeable existence.

Manonash results in this glorious state in which plurality goes and Unity comes, ignorance goes and Knowledge comes, binding goes and Freedom comes. We are all in this shoreless Ocean of Infinite Knowledge and yet are ignorant of it until the mind—which is the source of ignorance—vanishes forever; for ignorance ceases to exist when the mind ceases to exist.

Unless and until ignorance is removed and Knowledge is gained—the Knowledge whereby the Divine Life is experienced and lived—everything pertaining to the Spiritual is paradoxical. God, whom we do not see, we say is real; and the world, which we do see, we say is false. In experience, what exists for us does not really exist; and what does not exist for us, really exists.

We must lose ourselves in order to find ourselves; thus loss itself is gain.

We must die to self to live in God; thus death means Life. We must become completely void inside to be completely possessed by God; thus complete emptiness means absolute Fullness.

We must become naked of selfhood by possessing

nothing, so as to be absorbed in the infinity of God; thus nothing means Everything.

For these last four months, according to ordinary human standards and by ways and means known to Me, I have tried My utmost for the achievement of *manonash*, and I can say in all truth that I feel satisfied with the work done. This satisfaction is due to the feeling I have of having regained My old-life Meher Baba State—yet retaining My New-Life ordinary state. I have regained the Knowledge, Strength, and Greatness that I had in the Old Life, and retained the ignorance, weaknesses, and humility of the New Life. This union of the old and the new life states has given birth to Life that is eternally old and new.

The New Life period was a strange one for us in the West but we endeavored to keep together and hold meetings. My health was very bad and I had to have an operation. I hurried on with this as I had an intimation in 1951 that Baba was going to visit America and wished me to be there with Him.

He had asked Elizabeth and Norina to find a property in America where a center could be made ready for Him to visit and He set five conditions: the climate should be equable; it should have more than ample water; it should be virgin soil, never before built upon; it should be land that could be tilled; and it should be "given from the heart." After some searching Elizabeth found the ideal property in Myrtle Beach, South Carolina. In fact, it already belonged to her father and some business partners, and eventually he gave it to her as a gift. In a cable to Elizabeth, Baba said:

AM HAPPY TO FIND IN ALL YOUR LETTERS
ABOUT MYRTLE BEACH EVERYTHING THAT I
PERSONALLY AND SPIRITUALLY APPROVE OF
AND SANCTION. ALL MY LOVERS SHOULD
COOPERATE TO MAKE MYRTLE BEACH THE
SPIRITUAL ABODE FOR ONE AND ALL.

MEHER BABA

So in 1952, after postponing His promised trip in 1951, Baba
sent Donkin ahead to confirm that He was temporarily returning
to the Old Life and was coming to Myrtle Beach for the official
opening of the Meher Spiritual Center. Jean, at that time living in
the South of France, and I were the only ones invited from Europe
to attend the opening and, in fact, in the end she was too ill to
travel and I was the only one to be there from Europe.

I went over to New York on the *Queen Mary* and again stayed
with my cousin until Baba arrived with the *mandali*, the Eastern
women, Rano, and Kitty. Margaret and I went to greet them and
again it was like coming home and nothing mattered any more.
They were all very tired so we left after a short while, in the happy
anticipation of being with Baba for a long period. The next morning, together with Ruano, we joined them at the station. Elizabeth
had come up from Myrtle Beach and we all traveled together to
Florence, South Carolina, where several cars met us and took us
on to the center—so we were there from April 20.

A UNIQUE ATMOSPHERE

 We arrived at Myrtle Beach from Florence tired, but happy and excited to be in this special place filled with such love and that Elizabeth and Norina had worked so hard to prepare for Baba's visit. For me there was special happiness to be there for this official opening as I had been present for the opening of Meherazad. I remember my first impression of the center was driving through a canopy of pine trees to the two lakes and the private seashore beyond.

As it was not yet officially open, all those who had come to see Baba had to stay at various places in Myrtle Beach itself, except for Mehera, Mani, Goher, Meheru, Kitty, Rano, Elizabeth, Norina, and myself who stayed at the center. Margaret could only stay a short while because of her classes. Ruano, too, was only there a little time and Malcolm Schloss came for a week. Ivy Duce, her daughter, Charmian, Filis Frederick, Adele Wolkin, the Darwin Shaws, and Francis Brabazon came backward and forward as Baba gave daily interviews.

Baba wanted Gabriel Pascal to come to the center and I was

sent many times to make long distance telephone calls to Hollywood. Pascal, however, had other commitments and anyway he thought he would soon be seeing Baba as, after the stay at Myrtle Beach, a visit to California was planned. But Baba kept on and I got into the habit of saying, "Oh Lord, again?" whenever He asked me to phone once more. Mani picked this up and used to say laughingly, whenever I came into the room, "Baba, 'Oh Lord' is here!"

Pascal must have been sorry that he did not make just that extra effort to come down to Myrtle Beach as in the end the trip to California was canceled. He did see Baba again, and the film he was working on for Baba never came to fruition. Many years later, while seriously ill in a hospital in New York, he wrote his last typical "Pascal" letter to Baba:

> My Beloved Baba,
> I am like a new born boy starting to live again . . . I will bring my cameraman and my staff with me because I intend to do the two pictures, *Ghandi* and *The Slipper of a Perfect Master*, together. When You hear *The Slipper of a Perfect Master* You will laugh tears. A stroke of genius came in my mind to make Your picture in a completely revolutionary way. I will bring the scenario with me. It will be end of August in Your everlasting arms. I know You are always with me. . . .
>
> > Your always
> > faithful Phoenix,
> > *Gabriel*

During our stay we went for walks with Baba on the beach and, oh joy, played croquet—I as usual was not very good at hitting the ball the right way—and in the evenings Mani read extracts about the saints. Of course, Baba was very busy both with the preparations for the opening and the many new lovers who wanted to see Him; and we were busy helping. I was given a lot of correspondence to answer and Margaret and I went over the circular being printed to give to all those who were coming to Baba for the first time.

On the great opening day, Baba, the *mandali*, and Elizabeth were inside the big Barn and Rano and I stood at the entrance and announced people individually or in groups. Kitty had the task of taking the women in groups to visit the women *mandali*, which, of course, was a great joy to those in the West who had not met them before. It was a wonderful day. Elizabeth was marvelous. She had organized everything to run on oiled wheels and for her it was a triumph, but I felt so sorry for Norina. The opening was to have been the great moment for her and Elizabeth; the culmination of years of loyal and faithful work, but she was unwell and in the end had to be taken to a hospital and could not be there.

Murshida Duce and Charmian had been to India and met Baba before, and the Darwin Shaws, of course, were old disciples from 1932, as were Malcolm and Ruano. But this was the first meeting for so many, including Fred and Ella Winterfeldt, Filis Frederick, Adele Wolkin, and Francis Brabazon. I was pleased that Otelia Tejeira, one of the people I had told about Baba in Panama, had flown up to be there. Baba was so nice to her and said He would help her. She met Him again in 1956 in London, and was voted Woman of the Year in all the Americas in 1967. Baba had also promised Margaret that He would see some of her pupils from New York. Rushing to get there in time, they had to hire a small plane between them. As time went on and they did not arrive,

Baba sent everyone scurrying backward and forward but, eventually, almost at the deadline, they arrived after a troublesome and
dangerous flight, saw Baba, and became devoted to Him.

Baba gave many messages to the new and old lovers at this
gathering at Myrtle Beach, among them a helpful clarification on a
point which I know is one of the questions most often asked by
newcomers: "Why does God permit suffering?"

> Real Healing is Spiritual Healing whereby the soul
> becoming free from desires, doubts, and hallucinations,
> enjoys the eternal bliss of God.
>
> Untimely physical healing might retard spiritual
> healing. If borne willingly, physical and mental suffering
> can make one worthy of receiving spiritual healing.
>
> Consider mental and physical suffering as gifts from
> God which, if accepted gracefully, lead to everlasting
> happiness.
>
> God has been everlastingly working in silence, unob-
> served, unheard except by those who experience His
> Infinite Silence.
>
> If My Silence cannot speak of what worth would be
> speeches made by the tongue? The very moment when
> He thinks My speaking will be universally heard, God
> will make Me break My Silence.
>
> God is not to be learned or studied or discussed or
> argued about. He is to be contemplated, felt, loved, and
> lived.

This time, of being with Baba in such a beautiful place, was
a dream come true for all—newcomers and old. Baba said of

Myrtle Beach:

> Ages ago this was a place where I moved about and stayed and the combination of the lake, the ocean, and the woods gives it a unique atmosphere.

As the visit drew to an end, the men *mandali*, with the exception of Sarosh, were sent in advance to Meher Mount in Ojai, California, where Baba and the rest of us were to join them. We started off in two cars—Baba, Mehera, Mani, and Meheru in the first car driven by Elizabeth; and in the second, driven by Sarosh, were Kitty, Rano, Dr. Goher, and myself.

PERSONAL DISASTER

Baba had once warned that an accident would befall Him, but no one had given it serious thought. On this fateful day He told those of us in the second car, again and again, to keep up with the first car and not to get lost as He would never forgive us. As we all knew the final destination I suppose we did wonder why He was making such a fuss, but we had no intimation as to what was about to happen. When, on May 24, we reached Oklahoma—in the heart of America—our car was late for the rendezvous and we were getting anxious. Suddenly we came upon a group of people on a grassy bank and saw Baba and the women lying there. Sarosh said, "Oh, my God, there's been an accident!"

The car had been in a head-on collision with another driven by a disabled Korean War veteran. Baba, Mehera, and Meheru had been thrown out of the car and injured. Baba and Mehera were the most seriously injured, Mehera with head injuries and Baba with a broken leg and arm. Elizabeth was also badly hurt with broken arms, wrists, and ribs. But Mani, who had been sleeping, seemed unhurt and so were the occupants of the other car.

Horrified, we rushed to the spot and I recall so vividly the extraordinary expression on Baba's face—His eyes not seeing the immediate, but far away. He said nothing, did nothing but let everything be done to Him. He had once said that He would shed blood on American soil and here, from His head injury, He was bleeding freely on the ground. I had with me a little pillow and I gave it to Sarosh to put under Baba's head and so it became stained with His blood. (A few years later I gave it to someone going to America to take to Myrtle Beach for safe keeping as I felt it really belonged there.)

An ambulance took Baba, Mehera, and Elizabeth to a small, private hospital in Prague, Oklahoma, where a splendid doctor and staff did everything possible for them. Kitty and Rano stayed at the hospital to help with the nursing and the rest of us took rooms in a motel nearby.

Sarosh was in a terrible state: he was terribly worried that India would blame him for the accident and cabled to tell them the news and also telegraphed the *mandali* at Meher Mount, telling them to return immediately. He sent for Ivy Duce and Charmian who came with commendable speed and were towers of strength—giving advice on various points, and Margaret came down from New York as soon as she could. So, unexpectedly, we were all together again.

Every day we went to the hospital to see Baba and to inquire about Mehera. It was a privilege to be there at this period, and to share in any small way in Baba's suffering, suffering which He said was all the greater because of the injury to Mehera. This was the first time He allowed her to suffer physically and to share His suffering, and it must have had enormous spiritual repercussions in

the whole feminine world as well as a big influence on the relationship between the East and the West.

After Baba left the clinic the doctor/owner wrote a letter to
Him:

> ... from You and Your party we have seen a demon-
> stration of most of the teachings of Christ. Many
> Americans preach these things but we have never
> observed so close an application of them. The profound
> devotion to You which is demonstrated by all Your
> party convinces us that You deserve all of it. Such
> devotion cannot be forced, it can only be obtained by
> love; and to have that demonstrated affection from so
> many wonderful people is almost unbelievable. We are
> not accustomed to dealing with people who appreciate
> our efforts as You do and the manifestation of that
> appreciation leaves us very humble, with the feeling
> that we do not deserve it because we realize our limita-
> tions and faults. Therefore, instead of efforts being
> classed as work they have seemed a pleasure....
>
> *Ned Burleson, M.D.*

Baba, whose leg was heavily plastered, needed to recuperate
and so Donkin and Rano were sent on in advance to prepare
Elizabeth's house, Yaupon Dunes, at Myrtle Beach. Thirteen days
after leaving we returned to Myrtle Beach: Adi Sr. driving Mani,
Gustaji, Meheru, and myself in a car and two ambulances bringing
Baba, Mehera, and Elizabeth, accompanied by Kitty, Margaret,
and Sarosh. We traveled day and night to cover the fifteen
hundred miles.

Elizabeth had a nurse brought in, Margaret was able to help in a constructive way by giving Baba special exercises and the rest of us helped in any way we could. We saw Baba every day, and although He was in pain, He was considerably improved. About the accident He said:

> The personal disaster for some years foretold by Me has at last happened while crossing the American continent, causing Me, through facial injuries, a broken leg and arm, much mental and physical suffering. It was necessary that it would happen in America. God willed it so.
>
> It brings to fruition the first part of the circular which said that until July 10th (in the Complicated Free Life), weakness would dominate strength and bindings would dominate freedom; but from July 10th, in My Full Free Life, strength would dominate weakness and freedom would dominate bindings, and then from 15 November, in My Fiery Free Life, both strength and weakness, freedom and bindings, would be consumed in the fire of Divine Love.

In July, Margaret and I had to leave; Margaret for work and I because I had a reservation on the *Queen Mary*. Kitty was also returning to England, Baba allowing her to visit her family. Despite the accident He still meant to keep to His plan and visit London, and so on my return the League had a long meeting in order to make suitable arrangements. We booked a suite at the Rubens Hotel for Baba and the others, and I also booked a room there for myself so that I could be at hand at all times. Margaret had given me some money for tickets so that Baba and the women could see some shows while in London and so I booked several, including *South Pacific, Rose Marie*—on ice, a horse show for Mehera, the circus, and a second visit to the "Q" Theatre to see Richard Atten-bourough in a comedy.

Baba and the party arrived in London in August 1952. Although He was getting about with great difficulty Baba insisted on coming to all the evening entertainments so as not to disap-point Mehera and Mani—Mehera was much better and looked almost her old self again. Charmian Duce had also come over and one day Minta took her in her car to Stratford-on-Avon where the three of us had a lovely day together. On another day, I took Mehera and Mani to Madame Tussaud's waxworks and they also came to my flat at Kew, going for a walk in the Botanical Gardens before having lunch in a little restaurant in Richmond.

Baba had not been to England since 1936 and so there were many new people waiting to see Him, among them Fred Marks, Dorothy Kingsmill (who brought Tom Hopkinson), Molly and Douglas Eve, and many others. Tom Hopkinson had been editor of the Picture Post until 1950 and at that time was working at the News Chronicle. Will had arranged for interviews to be given in the mornings at the Charing Cross Hotel. After five days in London, Baba and the party left for Zurich on August 6 and to my joy Baba told me that I was to go with them. We were seen off at London Airport by many devotees—this was the first time I had traveled in a plane with Baba and I found it very exhilarating. He bore all His disabilities so patiently but, as He had so often explained, the Christ (Avatar) takes on suffering to redeem humanity.

Everything was wonderfully arranged: Irene Billo, who had

spent the war years in India with Baba, met us at Zurich and we motored to Locarno, having an excellent lunch on the way. We stayed at Hedi Merten's house. I shared a room with Charmian and we got to know each other well. (In fact, later Baba permitted her to come and stay with me in London.) Although many visitors came, including Roger and Anita Vieillard, it was still an intimate and wonderful two weeks. By now Baba was walking on crutches and we saw a lot of Him, especially in the evenings when Mani would often read spiritual poems or stories of the saints.

Baba and His group, except Kitty, were flying back to India from Geneva Airport. Kitty was not taken back this time as Baba told her to stay at Myrtle Beach and help Elizabeth. Of course, Baba knows what is best for each and what each needs, and Kitty has found a special niche there and is greatly loved. Everyone speaks of the wonderful work she does for Baba.

Charmian and I drove with Baba to the airport. My plane left before His, so I had to take a sad and reluctant farewell and He pointed out to me that I was the only one who had been with Him all through this Western trip. I did not know it then, but this was almost the last of these special intimate times with Him, for more and more His prediction of the large crowds that would come to Him was to be fulfilled.

THE TIME OF THE NEWCOMERS

 I did not see Baba again until 1956 when He traveled to London via Zurich, again on His way to America. In 1954 He had held a *sahavas* in India but it had been for men only. Charles Purdom, Fred Marks, and Will Backett had gone as well as several from America, among them Malcolm Schloss who, I was sad to hear, died shortly after returning to New York.

Baba was met at the airport in 1956 by many people. He had now discarded the alphabet board and was using only hand signs interpreted by Eruch and it was amazing how Eruch understood exactly what Baba wanted to say. We had again engaged a suite at the Rubens Hotel for Him. The Haefligers and Hedi Mertens had traveled with Him from Europe and Anita and Roger flew over from Paris to join Him, Anita amusing Baba as usual.

There had been differences between us on the committee of the Spiritual League and we asked Baba if He would preside at a meeting while He was in London, which He did. He allowed us to air our grievances, thoroughly but without bitterness. Will blamed

Charles and myself and said that we had tried to usurp his position which had made him ill. I did feel that perhaps I should have given way more and I was relieved to get it all out in the open. Baba let us have it out and then He told us to go away and come back later for His ruling.

When we reconvened, Baba said that this was our last chance and that we were to clasp hands and say that we would try and cooperate. We were given a copy of *What Baba Means by Real Work*, which He had given to other groups who were having similar difficulties:

> What I want from all My lovers, is real and unadulterated love...Love Me wholeheartedly, the time is near that the only thing which will count now is Love. That is why I have been telling you all to love Me more and more. Love Me, and then you will find Me. From you I want no surrender, no mind, no body, only love....

He appointed Will, Charles, and myself to have six-month periods as chairman in turn. He said that if during these periods any dispute arose, in or out of the committee, and we could not come to a decision, the chairman of the day was to give a ruling and we were to take it as if it came from Baba Himself. He also asked Dorothy Hopkinson to be secretary and treasurer which she accepted gladly.

On this visit, Baba said that He wanted to meet as many people as possible. We had arranged therefore an afternoon and evening reception together with an entertainment of singing and dancing so that as many people as possible could meet Him.

Dorothy was now married to Tom Hopkinson, editor of Picture Post, and together they created a canopy of flowers to surround Baba's seat where Will, Mary, and Charles sat by Him. Dorothy, Tom, and I showed people in and out—Baba looking radiant as He greeted each one so lovingly.

He explained that when in seclusion He did not normally give discourses and messages but, because of His love for us, He did give the following to these gatherings:

> One who hears the music of God in his heart, such wonderful music, for it is *the Original Music*, loses his bodily consciousness and sees God everywhere.
>
> God is within everyone. He is in all of us—Infinite, All Powerful. The helplessness that you feel now, here as you are in the body, is all illusion although God is so omnipotent. Why is that? It is illusion. It is the veil between you and God. The veil of what? That veil is the veil of ignorance. Once you come to know that the body is not real and this body is not you, then that veil of ignorance is lifted. When you are indeed asleep, the body is there although *you* are not.
>
> The body breathes and yet you are not aware of its breathing when you are asleep; then you may dream you eat, or in the dream you go to the pictures. It is not the body that dreams. It must be something that dreams; it must be YOU. Suppose this body has its legs cut off; you are in no way less conscious nor do you feel that there is any curtailment in your own existence. You are still *you* and your consciousness is not curtailed. Mind understands, yet the veil of illusion is not lifted

because of the veil of ignorance which you still have.

Once you see God within you, you get that conviction (of God). There is no more doubt. Then there is the experience of infinite bliss.

I give My blessing to you all.

If those who love Me will just for one minute, as now, be silent in their minds just before they go to bed and think of Me and picture Me in the silence of their minds, and do that regularly, then this veil of ignorance that they have will disappear and this bliss that I speak of and which all long for, they shall experience.

This visit was characterized by the hundreds of people who flocked to see Baba; my brother, Jack, who had nearly died the year before, came twice and Baba embraced him lovingly. He died very shortly after this meeting and Baba sent me a consoling cable: "BABA BEING FOND OF JACK, KNOW JACK IS IN GOOD HANDS." Minta and her husband came and another brother and nephew; Edmund Purdom, Charles' son, came twice; Molly and Douglas Eve and Joyce Bird; there were also several Indian disciples who now lived in London, including Baba's brother Adi and his wife, Franee. To these people who came, Baba gave His "prasad" of which He said at the time:

You all will have received from Baba what in India is called *prasad*, and that is not just a conventional gift. In India, where people gather in tens of thousands at a time to receive gifts from Him, something to eat like a sweet, they accept it as something great. When they go away, they realize that they have something of His Self, given as something from His own Heart. Because this present of *prasad* is really a seed of love planted in your heart, you should take that sweet with that idea in your mind when meeting Baba.

In spite of the crowds it was still a lovely two days—on the second there was a tea party for the more intimate ones. I felt so sad that I was not going with Baba to America and I told Him so. He said He would have suggested it if He had known I could have paid my fare, but of course I knew that if He had really meant for me to go it would have happened somehow.

Mary, Anita, and I went in the car with Baba to the airport and during the journey Baba said to Mary that when she passed on she would be with Him forever. At the airport a large group had gathered to see Him off and, once again, sadly we had to say goodbye. Those in America had the joy of traveling round with Him from Myrtle Beach to California. Although I was not there, I was with them in spirit as at a large reception held for Baba at the Manhattan House Hotel in New York, one of my poems, *The Beloved* was read out:

> Thy tender look
> Hath drawn my soul
> And set my heart
> Aflame with love
> For Thee always;
> Thou hast bestowed
> So much on me
> Unworthy me—
> My prayer shall be

To do Thy will
And more and more
To love Thee still
Until at last
I cease to be
And merge within
Thy love, so still.

After America Baba went to Australia, and on returning to
India He was involved in a second car accident in which Dr. Nilu
was killed and Baba quite severely injured. We were kept in touch
with the news of what was happening in India during these long
periods of absence by the *Family Letters.* These Baba authorized
Mani to send out each month to group heads around the world
who then distributed them among Baba lovers in their area. (These
were eventually published in a single volume.) They were full of
news and humor and were greatly appreciated and avidly read by
us all.

Those of us working for Baba in England did our best to work
cooperatively together. Dorothy left with Tom for Kenya where
he became editor of the Drum. Adi Jr. became the new secretary of
the League, and Douglas Eve came onto the committee as treasurer, where he worked devotedly for Baba until his death.

Baba had recovered sufficiently by 1958 to come over once
again for *sahavas* at Myrtle Beach. Neither Will nor Mary were
well enough to go but several from England did, including Fred
Marks, Joyce Bird, Charles Purdom, Hilda Thorpe, and myself.
Hedi Mertens came over from Switzerland and I met Anita in New
York and we traveled down together.

Now Baba's words kept coming back to me more and more

that we would not get near Him for the crowds. The center was full of new and old lovers greeted by Baba at the Lagoon Cabin, again He was giving us a unique outpouring of love. Every day we went to the Barn and He sat amongst us. Often music was played and I remember the radiant expression on His face when we played *He Has the Whole World in His Hands* or *Begin the Beguine*, which was always one of His favorite tunes and one which He said had spiritual meaning. Again He gave many interesting explanations for those who wanted them and one day He made us all stand and say the Prayer of Repentance. He made a sign of blessing and said all our sins were forgiven up to that date. Then it was done again for the absent ones.

We went on several walks down to the beach, an unforgettable experience being with Baba on the beach with the lapping waves and the happy crowd around Him. But Anita and I were having a taste of the aloof treatment which, from Baba, was a little hard to bear. Day after day went by and we were just in the crowd and seemed to be ignored. Others were called to spiritual interviews, but we were left out. This is a general experience some time or other for most Baba lovers. Of course, Baba knew how we felt, and I too came to understand that this was the time of the newcomers. However, near the end of the visit, we were called to the house and Baba gave each of us a photo of Himself selected by Mehera. He said we should not worry if He called one and others not at all; it was His way of working and He wanted from us love and obedience 100%. On the spiritual path, there is no room for compromise; and when we suffered, we were not to worry but say it was Baba's grace.

Again He cut short His trip by a few days, but asked those of us who could to stay on at Myrtle Beach in His absence. We were told to write Him one letter on our return home. The morning He was leaving, Kitty, Margaret, and I went over to see Him. He was alone and just for a few seconds we stood there and He put His hand to His heart and made a gesture of love to the three of us.

A large crowd was at the airport to see Him off and it was difficult to realize He would soon be gone again. Anita and I returned to Myrtle Beach as He had requested and then broke our journey home, and stayed two days in Washington, where I saw my cousin and visited some of the Sufi group.

Back in England, Mary and Will were failing and they did not see Baba again. They had given Him long and devoted service and I felt very sad for Will when Mary passed away first—she was a lovely soul and very dear to Baba. Will missed her terribly, sold up the house and went to stay with Maud Kennedy at Oxford, but he did not long survive his wife.

There were other changes in the English group. Molly and Douglas Eve had taken over as secretary and treasurer, as Adi Jr. had left the Committee, and for some years I was one of the editorial advisors to *The Awakener*, a magazine dedicated to Baba that Filis Frederick had started printing in America. My role was basically only an advisory one, but in the spring/summer edition in 1957, I wrote the following editorial: *Thoughts on the Master*:

> During the past weeks, in thinking of Baba's teachings, it became clearer than ever to me that it is not what Baba says, but what He is that is of such supreme value to us; for it is only when the words are backed by example that they carry conviction and have importance. Therefore, it is because Baba is here with us and gives us the example of His own life, that words and

teachings become transformed into living truth, and our hearts stirred and awakened. He shows us not only what we can become, but the love of God in manifestation. We see love, wisdom, and power in action and by His perfection we can measure our imperfection, and so be helped to a standard of true values. So the first thing that Baba teaches or wants of us is not to talk, but to do. . . .

It is for our sakes that Baba is here, for He is already perfect, and that He willingly endures limitation and suffering. Our receptivity to Him will help us to transcend our limited selves, for Baba, by holding Himself up for our attention and saying, "Read Me," shows us the meaning of perfection when man becomes God, and God becomes man—and also shows us what it means to function as a human being with complete balance, poise, and equilibrium. This is teaching in the truest sense, for He has trod every step on the path He asks us to take.

While Baba helps all humanity, His concern is with the individual, for perfection is an individual matter which each one has to attain personally. He says we must learn by our own efforts and conscious experience, but when we make the effort, He will give us the victory. That is why, with His close disciples, Baba has always been reluctant to give explanations. He points out that explanations and discussions do not help us to realize Truth—and when you experience it you do not need explanations.

For progress, the chief requisite is to love God sincerely, and with singleness of purpose. This is the cornerstone of Baba's teaching, for it is by love and through love that perfection is attained; but we are told, "True love is no game for the faint-hearted and the weak." We need courage, discipline, and a burning determination to let nothing deflect us from our chosen path.

To make clear to us the intrinsic worth of every human being He tells us, "God is in everything and everybody—you must feel in your heart of hearts that God alone is real, that He is the innermost self of all selves." He says this again and again in various ways—it is a basic statement in His teachings; for until we can really feel this we cannot understand the fundamentals of human relationships, nor know that when we hate or hurt anyone we are really doing it to ourselves.

Baba does not only talk of love, He enfolds all with the warmth of His own all-embracing love. Those who have met Him know the unique experience of being in the presence of someone who radiates pure love, and who makes you feel that whoever you are and whatever you have done, He really loves you and wants you to love as He does, and it is this love of Baba that melts the hard crust of our limited egos.

INTO THE '60s

From 1958 to 1962 Baba was in seclusion. We were asked not to disturb Him in any way during this time, but we did receive birthday messages and also, of course, Mani's *Family Letters* full of intimate news. In June 1960, a circular was sent out exhorting us all to hold fast to Baba's *damaan* under all circumstances to the very end. During this period I lost my second brother, Roy, and Minta, her husband. It was not until early 1962 that we had the certain news that there was to be an East-West Gathering in India; the message stated that this was to be a *"Darshan Sahavas"* for lovers from all over the world, taking place in November 1962.

Several of us went from England, including Charles Purdom and Mary Parry. I went by sea with Fred Marks and Molly and Douglas Eve. I carried with me 1,000 copies of the booklet, *Sparks*, as a gift for Baba from the West. This was a compilation of Baba's sayings. I had compiled it with great encouragement and help from Kitty, Charles had written the introduction and helped with the editing, and the project had been jointly financed by the English and American groups.

The Eves got off at Karachi to join us later at Poona, while Fred and I went on to Bombay where we were met by Arnavaz Dadachanji. Fred was told he was to go straight to Poona but I was to stay in Bombay until Enid Corfe arrived. The Dadachanji family was very kind to me and had me to a meal every day during my stay there. When Enid arrived, Meherjee drove us down to Poona. Although Baba was there He would not see anyone until all of us had arrived. So we stayed at the Poona Hotel while we waited the arrival of the rest of the group from America and Australia. They stayed at various hotels in Poona, and when Anita arrived with Charles Purdom, she shared my room.

Then the day before the *sahavas* was due to begin, there came a summons for Kitty, Elizabeth, Margaret, Delia, Anita, Ivy, Filis, and Adele to go and see Baba. He greeted us lovingly and we again had the joy of being in His presence. Although He was now walking after the accident, His hip still gave Him trouble and we were all conscious of His suffering.

In the afternoon we were taken to see Baba's family house, His old school and college, and Babajan's Shrine. Then we were called to meet Mehera, Mani, and the others. As always, it was a joy to be with them. No one had changed—Mehera was as lovely as ever and Mani was her usual bubbling self.

The *sahavas* was being held at Guruprasad, the spacious home of the Maharanee of Baroda that she made available for Baba's use each summer. It was a fitting setting for such a unique gathering. A large tent had been erected in the garden, gay with colors, with a platform where Baba sat, while we all sat on chairs facing Him. This was our first experience of a mixed gathering on such a large scale. Filis and Charles took notes, many took photographs, and there was some filming as speeches were given, music and *arti* performed, and messages from Baba read aloud.

On the first day it rained heavily and some of us were soaked. Baba gestured that we should go behind the platform to the room from where Mani, Mehera, and the other women were watching the proceedings. There, with their usual loving concern they brought out other garments for us to change into, Elizabeth being given a dress she had left behind after her stay in India ten years previously. It was unusual that it should rain at this time of the year, and we can only guess at the spiritual significance of this giving of garments from the East to the West.

In the mornings it was arranged for the Western group to come on their own to be with Baba in the large sitting room at Guruprasad, and there were music and talks and on certain days we were allowed to see Mehera and Mani and the others. Although the lovely intimacy of the early days was gone forever, we were witnessing a unique outpouring of Baba's love as can only be comprehended by those who were there. Day after day, East and West joined together to sit gazing rapt at this tireless and unprecedented outpouring of love and blessings.

For the first time in ten years, Baba allowed everyone to bow down and touch His feet—East and West, men and women, and the *mandali*. I filed past with everyone else remembering the only other time I had fallen at Baba's feet and He had gently pulled me to my feet, waggling His finger to indicate that I was not to do that.

On the day open to the general public, ten thousand people came, some from great distances; whole villages came—children and aged people and gypsies included. They filed past Baba and He greeted each one by touching them—spiritually taking their burdens on His shoulders. Still it went on; Baba was almost smothered with flowers, and most of us watching were in tears.

Again Baba shortened His stay, but He asked those of us who could, to stay and join the excursion to Meherabad and Meherazad. The last morning He embraced each of us individually and we made our farewells to Mehera and Mani. On the morning He left we assembled by the river in Bund Gardens to have one last glimpse of Him as He left, and as His car drove by He smiled and waved at us. It was sad because we were all getting older and we were well aware that some of us might not be destined to see Him again, but we knew we had seen and received the Word made flesh in all its glory. Later as I said goodbye to Margaret, she said, "I don't think we'll see Baba again." I must admit at that time I did not feel that way—it seemed unbelievable that Baba should leave us, but perhaps it was that I could not face up to the possibility at that time.

After the *sahavas*, I returned by sea to England with the Eves. Back in London, Charles Purdom was gathering material for his book, *The God Man*, but he was already an ill man. I certainly did not realize how ill he was and that his life was slowly drawing to a close, though he still had time to pay another visit to America, give many talks, and realize his dearest wish: to finish the book and arrange for its publication.

Again Baba had asked us to write one letter after our return and on April 6, 1963, I received a cable:

HOW ARE YOU? MY LOVE TO YOU.
BABA

In 1964, there was talk of another *sahavas* but it was put off. It was in that year I experienced the sad loss of my mother who was killed in a car accident on July 10—the day remembered by Baba lovers as the anniversary of the day in 1925 that Baba began His silence. It was a great shock, happening so suddenly in this way, but I was consoled by Baba, who in His great compassion sent me a loving cable:

BE BRAVE AND REMAIN RESIGNED TO DIVINE WILL. BE COMFORTED IN KNOWLEDGE THAT YOUR LOVE FOR ME HAS BROUGHT YOUR MOTHER TO ME. I SEND MY LOVE TO YOU ALSO MINTA AND FAMILY.

MEHER BABA

My relations in Panama offered me a trip to cheer me up and in February 1965 I went down there for three months. I went by sea via Miami, where it was a great pleasure to meet the Baba group and be with them for one evening. I returned to London via New York, staying a few weeks and was able to see the Baba Room at the World's Fair organized so efficiently by the American group. I met again Dr. Harry Kenmore and visited and spoke at the center there. As usual, all those I met were kind and friendly.

I spoke to Kitty and Elizabeth by telephone as I could not manage to go down to Myrtle Beach and it was also heartening to see the Winterfeldts, Enid Corfe, and others once again. But, of course, the greatest joy was when Margaret and I got together to talk of old times—the link never breaks. She, like Kitty, is a rock of strength and love for Baba.

I returned to England and attended our group meeting. I found Charles Purdom looking very ill, but it was still a shock to hear soon after that he had been taken to a hospital for an operation from which he did not recover. His death was a great personal loss as he had been a loyal friend and adviser for more than thirty years. He worked for Baba selflessly and left behind his books, especially *The God Man*, as a fitting memorial to an outstanding disciple in his depth of knowledge and understanding love for Baba. With his death I was now left alone as the last chairman appointed by Baba.

In 1965, some cousins took me on a trip to Greece and Israel. I fell in love with Greece, a beautiful country, and felt the extraordinary mystery of that land, especially at Delphi. In Israel, I was impressed by the energy of the Israeli people and there I met Carrie Ben Shamai, who told me about her work for Baba. I met her group and she came on several excursions with us. When we visited the room of the Last Supper, it seemed very familiar to me—I have always felt a love for Jesus as if I had seen Him and followed Him. Once, when asked if He would visit Palestine, Baba said that He was always there.

In 1967, Baba told us that the time was short and that He would be in strict seclusion. No one was to write to anyone except on business and no one was to contact Him except for His work. He again instructed us to hold fast to His *damaan* whatever happened.

The Baba scene in Britain in the early sixties had become rather disheartening. Apart from the Christmas Social and the celebration of Baba's birthday, the attendance at meetings became less and less. Douglas Eve became seriously ill and Molly could spare little time from nursing him for committee work. He did not recover from this illness and afterward Baba cabled Molly that not only was He pleased with the way she had looked after Douglas, He was proud of her!

Apart from Joyce Bird, who was the treasurer and efficiently managing our funds, I was more or less running things on my own. Fortunately, the Hopkinsons returned after eight years' absence to live in England and agreed to come back on the committee. And at this point in the summer of 1967, there was a sudden influx of young people.

It started one summer afternoon at our monthly Saturday meeting, when four of us were sitting rather disconsolately in a room we rented at the Poetry Society. Halfway through there was a knock at the door and four, what seemed to me, strange looking young people burst in—Martin and Christine Cook, Dudley Edwards, and Michael McInnerney. Michael and Dudley were working together on a design for a Chelsea tea shop called *The Flying Dragon*. They had seen an article and a photograph of Baba in a magazine called *Image* and Michael felt he wanted to know more about Him. Coincidentally, Dudley knew Martin Cook who, through a friend of his mother's, Mary Parry, had been hearing about Meher Baba all his life, but up to that time had not taken much notice.

A little taken aback, we did our best to make them feel at home and asked them to take part in reading some of Baba's messages, but I sensed we made little impression. Dudley told me afterward that as he went out he had said, "There's nothing for us here, we must find Baba our own way." Many years before, Baba had told me in a letter to act on my intuition and I would always be guided. I had had the presence of mind to take their address and that night I felt inspired to write to them and invite them to come and see me and hear more about Baba.

Within two weeks eight came along, including Katie, Michael's wife, and Mary Parry herself. We spent a pleasant afternoon looking at photographs and talking about Baba. Katie sat by me and there was an immediate bond of affection and understanding between us. This was the first of many more exhilarating afternoons and evenings. I felt as if Baba had taken me by the scruff of the neck and plunged me into a hippie atmosphere of music, laughter, parties, cups of tea, and Baba talk. It was strange to me that not only did I feel a deep sympathy with them, but completely at home as if I had known them for ages past, though I had never met their like before. I found that they all had had drug experiences—heroin, pot, LSD—and most of them had very little sense of time, but I soon adjusted to this and learned to ring up afternoons instead of mornings and also to say an earlier hour than the time I wanted them to be there.

The next move was that Michael, Katie, and Dudley took a large flat near the river in Richmond. From then on the pace quickened. They brought round friends or I went to them—I was always amazed at the enormous amount of social contact the McInnerneys had; they could produce large numbers of diverse people at very short notice.

One evening Dudley and Michael took me to show a film, photos, and to talk and distribute circulars at The Flying Dragon, and so I met some more of those who afterward became interested in Baba, especially Barbara Morice (now Frelje), part owner of the Dragon, who has since become a devoted Baba lover. There followed a burst of energy and creative activity of artists, musicians, poets, and writers, culminating in Pete Townshend, of The Who pop group, offering his studio in London's Wardour Street for Baba work.

I sent Mani the *Observer* color magazine which one week carried the story of The Who and had a photograph of Pete and the others on the cover. While Mani was looking at it, Baba came into the room and put His hand on Pete's face. Subsequently Mani gave Pete this photograph when he visited India. Apart from my sympathy with Pete, I always felt he had special work to do for Baba and certainly he was a leading spirit in that early, eager, and creative group and was instrumental in bringing many young people, especially musicians, to Baba, including Ronnie Lane of the Faces pop group.

Pete loves Baba deeply and in my view his greatest achievement is probably his beautiful setting of *The Master's Prayer* to music and later the production of the film, O, *Parvardigar*, with this as the sound track. This film is most important as it shows Baba at different stages of His life, with the lepers, *masts*, at *darshan* programs, and with His devotees in different parts of the world.

India knew what was happening and Baba's guiding hand could be felt all the time. Michael and I went to look at the studio in Wardour Street as soon as it could be arranged. I took one look at it and knew it was the right place—a large airy room with oval windows letting in the light from all sides. There was a kitchenette and entrance space which became an office. With the approval of the committee, I gratefully accepted the use of it as a center.

Then started a period of hard work to get the place ready. It was at this stage that Naomi Westerfeldt came onto the scene. She was living in England, but had met Baba through Margaret Craske. She helped in every way she could. I even rode in front of a furniture van and helped cart things up the flights of stairs, and by the time of the official opening in August 1968, more and more young ones had been drawn into the fold. All the older members of the Baba group—Molly, Tom, Dorothy, and Maud Kennedy—rallied round and gave their experiences of Baba on the day of the opening, when about seventy people attended, including Baba's youngest brother, Adi, and his wife, Frenee.

As is often typical with Baba functions, nothing is plain sailing—a thunderstorm broke out and when I had read the dedication and we started to show the film as planned, there was a loud bang and that was the end of that. Refreshments were served early and all agreed that, in spite of all not going according to plan, it was a fine opening.

At this time, too, Don Stevens had been transferred by his company to England. Don, author of *Listen, Humanity* and *Listen, the New Humanity* and co-editor with Ivy Duce of *God Speaks* and *Discourses*, attended one of our gatherings and told us about the American scene where young people were coming in large numbers. Afterward he wrote to me and offered to give weekly *Discourses* sessions at the center, an offer which we gratefully accepted.

In the meantime, quite a community of Baba lovers was growing in the Richmond area: Pete and Karen Townshend had bought a house by the river in Twickenham and later Dudley had a flat on Richmond Hill; Ronnie Lane and his wife, Sue, in spite of initial disinclination, gravitated to a flat just over Richmond Bridge, a few minutes from Michael and Katie; and Barbara and Mike Morice were living near them. Was this indeed what Baba had foreseen and planned when He stood on the balcony of my mother's sitting room at the Star and Garter?

Some time before the opening of the center, Michael McInnerney had made the remark, "If you want Baba's work to spread to England, you should get Dr. Allan Cohen over; he speaks our language." So I contacted Don Stevens and asked him to approach Allan. This he did and Allan said he would love to come, and arranged his visit for a month from the middle of September 1968. Tom and Dorothy were leaving for America but before he went, Tom very kindly arranged a press conference for Allan and a special interview with Lionel Birch (Mandrake), a journalist with a weekly column in a leading Sunday newspaper.

Allan was one of the three young Americans Baba had given the task of working against drug abuse and Baba sent His blessings for the visit. So it got off to a flying start and Allan was able to do remarkable work, appearing on TV and radio and giving many lectures. At that time, Baba's influence was helping so many give up drugs.

A newcomer on the scene at this time was Hilde Halpern who came from America via Vienna and who became a friend and counselor to many of us. Other newcomers were Craig and Georgina San Roque, Michael da Costa, and others who rolled up at Wardour Street every week to attend Don Stevens' *Discourses* sessions.

Baba announced another *darshan* to be held from April 10 to June 10, 1969 at Guruprasad which, He said, would be His last *darshan* in silence, would be for all time, and would be given in a reclining position. He also said, "The time is near, it is fast approaching, it is close at hand. Today I say the time has come. Remember this!" But in spite of these hints, we never really understood and were busy making arrangements to go to India to be with Him.

It was a great shock when I heard on the morning of February 1 from Adi Jr. that he had received a phone call from India telling him that Baba had dropped His body on January 31. I kept saying, "It can't be true," and crying, I phoned around to everyone. It seemed as if the whole world had disintegrated. It was the unbelievable happening.

There was already a meeting arranged at the center to discuss plans for going to the *darshan*. Now, instead, I went around to see Adi and we went together to the meeting to break the news, remembering what Baba had said, "When I drop my body I will remain in all who love me, I can never die. Lovingly obey me and you will find me."

"...WITH ME AT THE END"

How I found myself on the plane with Adi Jr. bound for India and the entombment is nothing short of a miracle. Until a few hours before the plane took off, I had absolutely no intention of making the journey. Adi had telephoned me to say that he did not wish to travel to India alone, and that he had been trying to trace Don to see if he could travel with him. He was about to leave for the airport and gave me the flight number, asking me to do my best to trace Don. Up to that point, I still did not contemplate going.

I did not succeed in contacting Don, but I suddenly felt intuitively impelled to go myself. I was talking to Hilde Halpern and she asked, "Are you thinking of going?" "How can I," I said, "It's Sunday and I've only got £3 in my purse!" Half an hour later she phoned again and said Alain Youell would drive me to the airport in Don's car. Her daughter Maria came with us and she lent me a few extra pounds spending money. I left in such a hurry, with such little time to spare, that I only had time to throw a few things into a small bag and leave a short note for my family saying, "I've gone to India!"

I joined Adi and Frenee at the airport but when I tried to buy a ticket from Air India, they refused to take my check. Meanwhile, Adi had checked in and disappeared to board the flight. I had almost given up the whole idea when eventually Frenee managed to persuade the clerk to issue my ticket, pointing out that her brother worked for Air India and that she and Adi would guarantee my check. This left me just enough time, before the bus moved off for the plane, to throw myself in beside an astonished Adi.

Usually I am a very bad air traveler, but somehow I sailed through this flight, except that as we got off the plane at the first stop I fell and hurt my right hip. I remember this particularly as it was this hip I had an operation on later. I hardly noticed the long car journey from Bombay to Ahmednagar, I was too stunned to take in what was happening. I think Donkin met us at Poona and drove us to Meherabad where we were taken by Eruch into the Tomb which was to be left open for seven days so that Baba's devotees could pay their last respects. Sarosh was there and he invited me to stay with him and his wife, Viloo, at their home in Ahmednagar.

How glad I was, the next day, to be with Mehera, Mani, the *mandali*, and the large gathering that came to pay their last respects to their Beloved. Of the Westerners there were only Don Stevens, Dr. Kenmore, Rick Chapman, Allan Cohen, and Aneece Hassan—the Luck brothers arrived on the last day and stayed for some time. So does Baba's will manifest itself at all times in our lives, for some time afterward I heard that Baba had said years earlier, "Delia will be with me at the end!"

Every year Baba gave out a birthday message and He had already given His message for February 25, 1969 before He dropped His body. The *mandali* sent it out as usual:

> To love Me for what I might give you is not loving Me
> at all, to sacrifice everything in My cause to gain some-
> thing for yourself is like the blind man sacrificing his
> eyes for sight. I am the Divine Beloved worthy of being
> loved because I am love. He who loves Me because of
> this will be blessed with unlimited sight and will see Me
> as I am.

The *mandali* also carried out Baba's instructions and organized the *Great Darshan* which took place as planned at Guruprasad
from April 10 to June 10, 1969, when His lovers gathered from all
over the world to pay their respects and homage to their Beloved.
Baba had always said He would take this *darshan* lying down and all
those lucky enough to attend said they felt His presence very
strongly. From England went the San Roques, Barbara and Dallas
Amos, Dudley Edwards, Christine and Martin Cook, and later
Ronnie Lane and Katie McInnerney. Barbara Morice, who was in
California, went with the American group.

During the critical years after Baba dropped the body, it was
marked how the lives of many Baba lovers changed and matured.
Many married, took up different careers, and there were a number
of lovely and intelligent young children. Many felt the need to go
to India for spiritual refreshment and get renewed faith in Baba. Of
course there were personal problems all round, but many accepted
their responsibilities and so held on to Baba's *damaan*.

Upasni Maharaj, one of the five Perfect Masters associated
with Baba, once said, "When the men and women of the West sing
and dance in praise of God, the spiritual revival will take place."

Baba predicted that the young would come to Him in droves and so it has been. To India and Myrtle Beach they have flocked to take His *darshan* and lay their lives at His feet. They are the vanguard of the New Humanity that Baba said would come into this new age of intuition:

> Through Divine Love, the New Humanity will learn the art of cooperation and harmonious life; it will free itself from the tyranny of dead forms and release the creative life of spiritual wisdom; it will shed all illusions and get established in the Truth; it will enjoy peace and abiding happiness; it will be initiated in the life of eternity.

CHANGES

Since 1969, many changes have taken place: several of the young people came onto the committee and we moved the center just before Christmas 1969 to a large basement flat in Eccleston Square near Victoria Station, lent by Karen Townshend, as Pete wanted to dispose of the Wardour Street studio. For months a group of helpers had been cleaning and painting it. Karen had made curtains and new cushions and Molly had worked hard, helping with the packing up at Wardour Street and doing her share of painting. Then the usual happened. I got the flu and the removers let us down at the last moment. Michael Ward came to the rescue, organized another removal, and with a band of helpers (including Molly and Naomi) did the whole move in time for the dedication in January 1970.

Two of Baba's close *mandali* visited the West in February 1970: Adi Sr. and Meherjee. They spent two days in London and so many young people who were unable to go to India had the chance to meet them and hear their experiences. Later in the year, Rano Gayley came to London as part of a world tour, and was here for several weeks. She came and spoke at the center and visited many Baba lovers. Rick Chapman also came later in the year and made Baba known to many new people through his talks.

The most exciting and creative activity launched in 1970 was the *Disc Magazine*, a tribute to Baba, brought out on His birthday, February 25. With Pete and Ronnie in charge, this combined the talents of Dudley, Martin, Craig, Michael da Costa, John Horder, Michael McInnerney, and others. It was an instant success. In 1972, the second *Disc Magazine*, "I Am," was launched. This was not as successful as "Happy Birthday," mainly, I think, because the original formula of a magazine was changed into a newspaper. In 1972 came the solo album "Who Came First" arranged professionally by Pete. This went on general release and did extremely well, bringing Baba's name to a much wider audience. There was a third *Disc Magazine* in 1976, "With Love," edited by Martin Cook and Mathew Price. These projects were originally launched by Pete as a cooperative effort to help the English group's many talented young people to be active and creative.

I moved up Kew Road from 240 to 280, a large ground floor flat and garden, adjacent to Kew Gardens. This meant I could give garden parties each summer for any Baba lovers who wanted to visit the botanical gardens and also, at the suggestion of Barbara Amos, I started holding informal weekly meetings using Mani's *Family Letters* as a focal point. These were so successful that they have continued in one form or another ever since.

In autumn 1974, Murshida Ivy Duce, of Sufism Re-oriented, and her daughter, Charmian, and Charmian's husband, Duncan, paid us a visit. Pete arranged a large reception for them where Ivy and Charmian shared their experiences of Baba with us. One evening during their visit, as he drove me home, Pete broached the idea of my making a film telling stories of my experiences with Baba. I felt very diffident at my age, to launch on such a project, but again some deep inner guidance made me say, "Yes." The fact that Baba had told me in the 1930s that I would play a part in His film gave me the deep conviction that this was His way of working and it would lead to a wider and more important development in films. I wrote to Pete that he was embarking on something that was much bigger than he could then visualize.

To my horror, within four days, I was told the film crew would come to my flat to start—no preparations, no scenario, no discussion of questions. They turned up, plus Pete, Billy Nichols, Richard Barnes, and John Annunziato, a photographer who had arrived in London with his wife, Linda. I was recovering from an angina attack but managed to pull myself together, though how I stood up for two days to seven hours of interviewing I will never know.

Tom and Dorothy's book, *Much Silence*, was published by Victor Gollancz Ltd. in 1974 and they generously put the copyright in the name of the Meher Baba Spiritual League. This is a fascinating book and has been very successful. It is especially helpful for people asking about Baba for the first time and I have heard many people, particularly in America, say what a helpful introduction they found it.

I grew very impatient at the way the "Delia" film was going and felt I was being constantly fobbed off. I felt something had to be done and at last when the whole project seemed to me to be on the point of collapsing, I told Pete he should take hold of it himself. It had been given a great deal of publicity, particularly in America, and he should do something before it became a fiasco. So from that time it really became a "Pete-Delia" production, for Pete now became writer, director, and narrator.

In the early part of 1975, driven on by his love for Baba, Pete decided that the time had come to expand and amplify Baba's work in the UK and that there should be a place in the Richmond area dedicated to Meher Baba. After viewing several places, he took me to see the *Boathouse* in Twickenham. It was in such a very dilapidated condition that we had to climb ladders to view it. His deep instinct was to buy it and rebuild it according to his idea of a Baba center/workshop which would have living accommodations and a theater. Encouragement came from India and America, and I was happy to know this dream could at last come true.

I had given up the chairmanship of the Spiritual League and Don (and later for a short while Tom) had taken on the task. But around this time, I agreed to take on the chairmanship again, as well as being vice president, as there had been many internal conflicts and I hoped to be able to bridge gulfs and bring us all closer together. At this time there were two organizations dedicated to Baba's work in the UK: the Friends of Meher Baba and the original Spiritual League, which had its roots in the Circle Editorial Committee of the 1930s and which handled the financial affairs.

The first decision we made was to amalgamate these two organizations, and thanks to the patience and hard work of our then-treasurer-now-chairman, Laurie Kaye, this eventually came about. We were then able to go ahead with an approach to the Charity Commissioners to get charity status for the association, which was granted in September 1976. The Meher Baba Association, organized on the democratic lines that Baba deemed best and with Meher Baba still as president, became the main organization and focus for Baba's work in Britain.

I had not been to India since the entombment and I could not travel alone, so when an opportunity to go with Pete in October 1975 came up, I knew I could not miss it. For various reasons it was postponed, but we did eventually go in February 1976. Pete made all the arrangements and he looked after me very well, being incredibly patient which somehow always amazes me.

It was a joyful two weeks. I was given such a lovely welcome. We arrived the day before the seventh anniversary of Baba's entombment (Amartithi) and so were able to take part in this very special day and its prayers and songs. For me, it was a happy reunion with Mehera, Mani, and all the *mandali* which I had not expected to happen again. To spend time at Meherazad with them all is a unique experience. There in that lovely, peaceful place one feels strongly enfolded by Baba's love. I was fortunate to be there for my birthday, on February 10, and everyone made it a very happy occasion for me.

All were interested in the progress of Meher Baba Oceanic and gave Pete their whole-hearted support; and we came back with the happy assurance that, health permitting, Adi Sr. would come over for the dedication. As Pete and I sat alone in the Tomb that last morning to pay our final respects to Baba, he sang his own arrangement of the Master's Prayer, *Parvardigar*, and it seemed to draw the two of us together in a karmic bond, a moment that lingered in my mind many weeks after my return.

Meher Baba Oceanic was opened on July 3, 1976 with ten days of music, drama, films, and food. The films, all sponsored by Pete and produced at Oceanic, included one on Fred Marks made by Martin Cook and Dudley Edwards; a documentary on Kim and Anita made by John Annunziato; two films edited by Ginny Katz, *The East/West Gathering* and *O, Parvardigar*; and a film by David Carter, *Meher Baba in Italy*. In addition there were two short documentaries of Allan Cohen talking about Baba that had been made during his visit in May; and, of course, Pete promised me the "Delia" film would be shown. With so much to do, this meant he and John had to work sometimes all night to get it finished.

Among the hundreds at the opening, about twenty-five had met Baba, among them Anita, Baba's nephew and niece Dara and Shireen, Frenee, Kim, Fred, Dorothy and Tom, Molly and Ann Eve, the Haefligers, Enid Corfe, Hilde Thorpe, Joyce Bird, Minta, Ann Conlon, and, of course, our special guests Kitty and Adi. During those ten days, everyone seemed caught up in the spirit of international goodwill and a desire to do what they could to make it a success. From India, Mehera had sent a pink coat worn by Baba and a beautiful letter:

AVATAR MEHER BABA KI JAI!
Beloved Baba's dear children gathered here today, we your Meherazad family are very happy at this joyous occasion which inaugurates MEHER BABA OCEAN-IC made possible by Beloved Baba's Grace.

Pete Townshend's desire to create Meher Baba Oceanic, with its pure aims and ideals has been inspired by his love for his Beloved Master, Avatar Meher Baba. Working for Baba does not mean that things are smooth and easy, but when you are wholehearted in your endeavor to serve and please Him, Baba always makes it possible. He guides and helps you at every step. We are proud of you dear children, of your selfless dedication in the work that you do in Baba's Love.

Our dear Pete, in his love for Beloved Baba, has played a major role in constructing Meher Baba

Oceanic. It is now for you all to help make it Baba's Home, where you can gather and work in His Love, and feel that He is here with you and know that His beautiful presence surrounds you. It is also for you all to make Meher Baba Oceanic a happy and harmonious medium for others to be drawn to Meher Baba's precious Love.

May Avatar Meher Baba's Love and Blessings shower on you all on this special day. Love to you each His dear ones from your Meherazad family.

Lovingly in Beloved Baba's Infinite Love.

Mehera

Many new people were to come to Baba through Oceanic—my Tuesday night meetings transferred there and were lovely occasions—and a lot of work, especially with films, was done there. Pete also opened a book shop in Richmond where Baba books were sold to a much wider public.

In 1979, because of a lack of funds, the Association was forced to close the center at Eccleston Square. Pete kindly offered us the use of Oceanic for our weekly meetings and these were very successful. So along with Oceanic's own meetings and the yearly pantomime or play in the theater there, there was a busy schedule of Baba activities for the growing number of Baba lovers.

But Oceanic was very expensive to run, and through this and other problems Pete was forced to close it as a Baba center in 1981. This left the Association for a time without a home and we went back to holding our monthly meetings at hired venues such as the Friends Meeting House in Central London.

Naturally I was very upset at the loss of Oceanic and I was also having increasing difficulty walking. Eventually in 1984 I had to go into the hospital to have a hip replacement operation. As I lay in the hospital ward, helpless and alone, my legs suspended after the operation, the walls seemed to recede. I felt totally alone and I seemed to get a glimpse of the meaning of Baba's words: "God alone is real, all else is unreal! Only through Love is He found." I knew the "real" me was eternally safe in Baba's arms, as He said in His very first letter to me, "I am always with you, in you, and around you. I am your very own self."

That same year Don offered his flat in Hammersmith for the Association to use, which we gratefully did for twelve months. Then Maxine Summers was selling her flat, in the basement below Don's, and through her generosity and through other Baba lovers who contributed, we were able to buy it. At last through the work, dedication, and generosity of so many Baba lovers, the Meher Baba Association owns its own center where meetings are held, books can be bought, and films and videos about Baba are shown. In addition, throughout Britain, lively groups are forming: the Norwich Group has done very special work under Michael da Costa, being the first group to hold *sahavas* in England; and there are groups in Devon, Lancaster, and Oxford where Dorothy Hopkinson now lives. Tom Hopkinson died in July, 1990.

STILL IN KEW

I had hoped in my old age to spend my last days at a Baba center surrounded by other Baba lovers, although I knew that Myrtle Beach was not a possibility for me, and besides, Baba had left me in England.

I had had very happy times at my flat in Kew. In fact, in the early 1970s and 1980s, it was almost a Baba center. In another flat in the same building were at first the three Americans who were studying acting; then later Mathew Price, who became secretary of the Association while working for Eel Pie Publishing at Oceanic; then when Mathew married and moved out, Hilary Stabler took over the flat; and finally Shireen (Meher Baba's niece) and Jay Bonner occupied another flat. Their daughter, Mehera, was born while they lived there, and Shireen helped me start on my memoirs. There had also been my Tuesday evening meetings, and gatherings for Adi Irani, Sr., Meherjee Karkaria, Kitty Davy, Bhau Kalchuri, and other visitors—happy days—but finally I found myself the only tenant in a deserted house and my flat full of rising damp.

Although for some time I strongly resisted the idea of a retirement home because I did not like giving up my independence, I did start selling and giving away some of my possessions in early 1987, feeling that a new way of life was indicated. In the end I moved in November of that year to a retirement home, still in Kew. In a way I knew it was Baba's will and He heartened me, but I have always liked being with younger people and now I am facing old age with other older people, some much older than myself. Margaret Craske wrote many years ago, "Old age is not pretty and it needs fortitude and courage." In my case, it is teaching me tolerance and patience.

Nevertheless, I have made a few good friends at the retirement home and have told several people about Baba. My mood was lifted just at the right time by Karen Townshend who gave a dinner party for me just after the move. Also, spending Christmas Eve and New Year's with Baba lovers helped.

Some Baba lovers find it difficult to understand why I am not happy now, but while admitting this is only my personal ego putting up a struggle for its own idea of happiness, it would be hypocritical for me to say otherwise. And I do get exasperated by people telling me how I should be happy. But whatever happens it is Baba's will and it is for me to accept it and to try to understand and learn what, even at my age, Baba is still trying to teach me.

From the moment I met Meher Baba I had complete and utter faith in Him. He awakened me to love—to love Him, to love God—and through Him I came to like people more than I did before I met Him. From the start I knew it was my destiny to love, work for, and obey Him as best as I could. I know that you have to be prepared, as He says in the "Highest of the High" message, to "Never stretch out your hands to receive anything from me." I still have complete faith in Him and accept Him as the Avatar—the Savior.

I have a box of cards with sayings from Meher Baba printed on them which we use at meetings—each person picking one out— and it is surprising how often these are a great comfort, being exactly fitting for the occasion. One evening not long ago I selected this one which I think says it all:

> Do not get disheartened and alarmed when adversity, calamity, and misfortune pour in upon you. Thank God, for He has thereby given you the opportunity of acquiring forebearance and fortitude. Those who have acquired the power of bearing with adversities can easily enter the spiritual path.

BIBLIOGRAPHY

Readers who wish to know more about Meher Baba are referred to the following:

BOOKS

God Speaks by Meher Baba. The Theme of Creation and Its Purpose. First published in 1955. Dodd, Mead & Co., New York, 1973. Cloth.

Discourses by Meher Baba. These Discourses first appeared in the *Meher Baba Journals*, 1938–1942. Seventh edition published in 1987 by Sheriar Press. Paperback and cloth.

God to Man and Man to God, a one-volume edition of Meher Baba's Discourses edited and condensed by C.B. Purdom. First published in England in 1955 by Victor Gollancz; reissued in 1975 by Sheriar Press. Paperback and cloth.

The Everything and The Nothing by Meher Baba. Discourses given in the late 'fifties and early 'sixties, compiled by Francis Brabazon. Published in 1989 by Sheriar Press. Paperback.

The Perfect Master by C.B. Purdom. The story of Baba's life up to 1936. First published in England in 1937; reprinted in paperback by Sheriar Press, 1976.

The God-Man by C.B. Purdom. A full and rich biography of Meher Baba up to 1962. Published in England in 1964 and reprinted in 1971 by Sheriar Press. Cloth.

The Beloved: The Life and Work of Meher Baba by Naosherwan Anzar. A pictorial biography interweaving 165 photographs with a colorful text. Published in 1974 by Sheriar Press. Paperback.

Treasures from the Meher Baba Journals, compiled and edited by Jane Barry Haynes. An excellent selection from the 1938–1942 Journals including beautiful photographs of the life with Meher Baba during that period. Published in 1980 by Sheriar Press. Paperback.

Love Alone Prevails: A Story of Life with Meher Baba by Kitty Davy. An extraordinary, detailed 700-page account of Miss Davy's 50 years with Meher Baba. Published in 1981 by Sheriar Press. Cloth.

The Dance of Love, My Life with Meher Baba by Margaret Craske. Sixty-two stories told with wit, warmth, and love by one of Meher Baba's earliest western disciples, the noted ballet teacher Margaret Craske. Published in 1980 by Sheriar Press. Paperback.

Still Dancing With Love, More Stories of Life with Meher Baba by Margaret Craske. Published in 1990 by Sheriar Press. Paperback.

VIDEOS

Memoirs of the Frivolous Three: An Evening With Margaret Craske, Kitty Davy, and Delia DeLeon. 73 minutes taped in September 1988 in Myrtle Beach, featuring three of Meher Baba's earliest western disciples. VHS. Distributed by Sheriar Press.

Hello, Ducks. A 22-minute tribute to Margaret Craske, combining movie film, audio tapes, and still pictures. VHS. Distributed by Sheriar Press.

A Date With the Eternal Beloved: Amartithi in India 1989. 32 minutes of the major celebration of Meher Baba's life in India. VHS. Distributed by Sheriar Press.

There are many books by and about Meher Baba and many videos. For a free list or further information, contact: Sheriar Press, Book Division, 3005 Highway 17 ByPass North, Myrtle Beach, SC 29577, USA.

In the United Kingdom, contact: Meher Baba Books, Old Rectory House, Marston Magna, Yeouil, Somerset, England BA228DT.